THE

# LIFE AND CHARACTER

OF

# CALVIN,

## THE REFORMER,

## REVIEWED AND DEFENDED.

BY THE

### Rev. THOMAS SMYTH, D. D.

Author of Lectures on the Apostolical Succession, Presbytery and not Prelacy the Scriptural and Primitive Polity, Ecclesiastical Republicanism, An Ecclesiastical Catechism; &c.

---

Quid enim tota ejus vita nisi tempestas veluti quædam perpetua fuit ?—MORUS.

---

*Wipf and Stock Publishers*
150 West Broadway • Eugene OR 97401
2001

The Life and Character of Calvin, The Reformer, Reviewed

By Smyth, Thomas
ISBN: 1-57910-689-7

Reprinted by *Wipf and Stock Publishers*
150 West Broadway • Eugene OR 97401

Previously published by Presbyterain Board of Publication, 1844.

# CONTENTS.

### SECTION I.
Introductory remarks, - - - Page 9

### SECTION II.
Calvin was the most eminent of all the Reformers, and remarkable for his courage, 13

### SECTION III.
The genius and works of Calvin, - 19

### SECTION IV.
Calvin vindicated from the charge of ambition, and his true greatness and wonderful influence shown, - - - - 25

### SECTION V.
Calvin vindicated from the charge of illiberality, intolerance, and persecution, - 33

### SECTION VI.
Calvin vindicated from the charge of a want of natural affection and friendship, - 48

## CONTENTS.

### SECTION VII.

The obligations which we owe to Calvin, as American citizens and Christians, illustrated, - - - - 52

### SECTION VIII.

The closing scenes of Calvin's life, - - 59

### SECTION IX.

A supplementary vindication of the ordination of Calvin, - - - - 65

### APPENDIX.

The Will of John Calvin, - - - 81
The views of Calvin on Prelacy, vindicated by the Rev. Samuel Miller, D. D., - 87

ADDENDA, - - - - 115

## PREFACE.

THE fact that John Calvin was led, by the grace of God, to embrace and defend all the essential principles of doctrine and polity, which distinguish the system of Presbyterianism, has exposed him to the unceasing calumny of all those to whom that system is unpalatable. Romanists, prelatists, and errorists of every name, have vied with one another in their efforts to blacken his character and detract from his fame. The defence of Calvin against these misrepresentations is necessary for the glory of that God who called him by his rich grace; for the honour of that truth in whose cause Calvin lived and died; and for the maintenance of that church to which he was attached, and which is built upon the foundation laid by apostles and prophets, Jesus Christ himself being the chief corner stone. And this defence is in a peculiar manner the privilege and duty of Presbyterians, with whom Calvin has been so generally identified.

Actuated by these views, the alumni of the Theological Seminary at Princeton appointed the author to deliver a discourse in vindication of the life and character of Calvin, at their anniversary meeting in May, 1843. The substance of the following little work was accordingly delivered in Philadelphia, in the second Presbyterian church, during the sessions of the General Assembly. At the request of the alumni, it has since been published in some of our religious papers; and it is now prepared by the desire of the Board of Publication of the Presbyterian Church, for publication as one of their volumes.

That it may lead the members of our beloved church more highly to estimate and prize the character and achievements of Calvin; that they may thus be excited to bless God, (who raised up Calvin, and qualified him for his work) for his past dealings with his church, while they humbly look for his continued guidance and protection—and that the inhabitants of this country may be brought by it more deeply to appreciate the influence of Calvin, and of the system he advocated, in securing those blessings of religious and civil freedom by which they are distinguished, is the sincere prayer of

THE AUTHOR.

THE

# LIFE AND CHARACTER

OF

# CALVIN.

## SECTION I.

INTRODUCTORY REMARKS.

Presbyterians, that is, the great body of the reformed church throughout the world, have been very commonly denominated Calvinists. Not that they are followers of Calvin, either in doctrine or in discipline, since the doctrines and discipline embraced by Presbyterians existed previous to the appearance of Calvin, and were adopted, and not originated, by him. Calvin, however, being the great theologian of the reformers, so well defended, so clearly expounded, and so perfectly systematized these principles, as to connect with them, wherever they are known, his illustrious name. The term Calvinist was first employed in the year 1562, in reference to the standards of the Huguenots or French reformed churches, which Calvin drew up; from which time it came to be employed as characteristic of all those who adopted similar doctrinal principles.* These principles, however, no more originated with Calvin than did the Bible, for they are the very same which were held forth by the apostles —which were proclaimed in all the apostolic churches—which were maintained by the ancient Culdees, by the Waldenses, and by other pure and scriptural bodies—and which were eminently defended by the celebrated Augustine, and by other divines, in every period of the church.

As Presbyterians, we hold no principles which are not found in the Word of God. We claim no antiquity more recent than the primeval organization of the church of God on earth. In our Christian form, we build upon the only foundation laid in Zion, the foundation of apostles and prophets, Jesus Christ himself being the chief corner stone. We call no man master upon earth. We know no man after the flesh. We call neither Abraham, nor Moses, neither Paul, nor Augustine, neither Luther, nor Calvin, our father. We are in subjection to no man, nor do we wear the name or livery of any. We are Christians in doctrine, and Presbyterians in polity, our doctrine being deduced from the Scriptures, and Presbytery being the only polity known to the apostles, or to the apostolic and primitive churches of Christ.

But while we so speak, let us not be supposed to disparage the name and character

* Scott's continuation of Milner, p. 472.—Waterman's Life of Calvin, p. 210.

of Calvin, or to deprecate, as either shame or reproach, the application of the term Calvinists. In the great body of Calvin's principles—though not by any means in all—we concur. To the life, character, and conduct of Calvin, we look with reverence and high esteem. And while we apologize not for his errors, or his infirmities, yet were we required to be called by any human cognomen, there is perhaps no other man, since the days of the apostles, by whose name we would prefer to be designated.

The reputation and character of this distinguished reformer have been opposed by every artifice of ingenuity, sophistry, and malignity. The vilest and most baseless calumnies have been heaped upon his memory. The most senseless and improbable stories have been invented to blacken his character, and to detract from his illustrious fame. A single event, distorted, misrepresented, and in all its circumstances imputed to his single agency, although consummated by the civil authorities of the republic, and although in accordance with the established sentiments of the age, has been made to colour his whole life, to portray his habitual conduct, and to cover with infamy the man and his cause. Now, in these very efforts of his enemies, romish and prelatist, and in their nature, source, and evident design, we find a noble testimony to the genius, power, and worth of Calvin. He who opposes himself to existing customs and prevalent opinions, must anticipate resistance in proportion to the success with which his efforts are accompanied. And while such opposition, in itself considered, does not prove that such a man is right in his scheme of reformation, but only that his plan involves the subversion of established forms, yet may we learn the character of such an intended reformation, and of such a bold reformer, by the very nature of that opposition which is brought to bear against him. And if, as in the present case, we find that, in order to withstand the overwhelming influence of such a man, his enemies are driven to the invention of forgeries, and the grossest fabrications, we may with certainty infer, that his personal character was irreproachable. In like manner, when these enemies are led to meet the arguments of such a man, by personal invective and abuse, we may be equally assured that his is the cause of truth and righteousness, and theirs the cause of error. Truth is strong in her conscious and imperishable virtue. She seeks therefore the light, courts investigation, and offers herself to the most impartial scrutiny. Error, on the contrary, having no inward strength, is weak and cowardly. She seeks the covert and the shade. She clothes herself in the garments of concealment. She assumes borrowed robes and names, and seeks by artifice and treachery to accomplish her base designs. In Calvin, therefore, we have a tower built upon the rock, and rearing its lofty head to the clouds, visible from afar, and open to the observation of all men; which, though the floods roar, and the winds arise against it, yields not to the fury of the tempest—because its foundations are secure. In the enemies of Calvin, we behold the secret plotters of his ruin, who, sensible of his invincibility, when opposed by any fair or honourable onset, dig deep within the bosom of the earth, and there concealed by darkness, and buried from all human sight, ply their nefarious arts to sap and undermine, and by well concerted stratagem attempt to overwhelm in destruction, an innocent and unsuspecting victim.

## SECTION II.

##### CALVIN WAS THE MOST EMINENT OF ALL THE REFORMERS, AND REMARKABLE FOR HIS COURAGE.

"Calvin," said Bishop Andrews, "was an illustrious person, and never to be mentioned without a preface of the highest honour." "Of what account," says his great opponent, Hooker, "the Master of Sentences was in the Church of Rome, the same and more amongst the preachers of reformed churches Calvin had purchased: so that the perfectest divines were judged they, which were skilfulest in Calvin's writings; his books almost the very canon to judge both doctrine and discipline by." And again, concerning his Commentaries and his Institutes, which together make up eight parts out of nine of his works; Hooker adds, "we should be injurious unto virtue itself, if we did derogate from them whom their industry hath made great. Two things of principal moment there are which have deservedly procured him honour throughout the world: the one his exceeding pains in composing the Institutes of Christian Religion; the other his no less industrious travails for exposition of holy scripture, according unto the same institutions. In which two things whosoever they were that after him bestowed their labour, he gained the advantage of prejudice against them, if they gainsayed, and of glory above them, if they consented."

Such was the estimation in which Calvin was held by his cotemporaries, both continental and Anglican. To Cranmer and his associates in the English Reformation, he was all in all. They sought his counsel, leaned upon his wisdom, were guided by his directions, and sustained by his consolations. His name is found enrolled with honour in the book of convocation as late as the seventeenth century, and his spirit still breathes through those articles which have preserved the protestantism and the orthodoxy of the English church.[*]

Among the continental reformers, Calvin was equally pre-eminent. Giants as they were in intellect, in acquirement, and in prowess, he towered above them all, like

[*] Lond. Christian Observer, 1803—p. 143, 144.

Saul among the people of Israel. Where all were great, he was greatest. Though naturally less courageous than Luther, he was enabled to manifest a superhuman bravery, and was, even in this respect, not a whit behind this noble champion of the truth. "He was," says Bayle, "frighted at nothing." Exquisitely sensitive and timid by constitution, he was, from his earliest years, obliged to bend to the inflexible rule of duty, and thus became habituated to self-sacrifice. When God called him by his grace to the knowledge of the truth and power of the gospel, he took up his cross to follow Jesus, suffering the loss of all things, and not counting his life dear unto him. The storm of persecution was then at its height. Its fiery bolts were spreading consternation and alarm throughout all France. The parliament was on the watch. The spies of the Sorbonne and of the monks were found creeping into churches and colleges, and even into the recesses of private dwellings. The *gens d'armes* patroled the highways to hunt down every favourer of the reform.* Then it was that Calvin enlisted as a good soldier under the Captain of Salvation; buckled on the armour of God, and threw himself boldly on the Lord's side. His whole subsequent course proves that, through the grace of God, he was valorous even to daring. At the risk of

* See D'Aubigné's Hist. of the Ref. vol. 3. p. 643— Eng. ed.

his life, he ventured back to Paris, in 1532, in the very midst of abounding persecution, that he might defend the truth. While the whole city of Geneva was in a ferment of rage, he hesitated not to suspend the celebration of the communion, and when publicly debarred the use of the pulpit, to appear in it as usual. When the plague had broken out, and was carrying death and destruction around, Calvin hesitated not to offer himself as a chaplain to its infected victims. During his contests with the libertine faction, he frequently attended the summons of the senate, when his life was exposed to imminent danger from the swords of the contending parties, many of whom were anxious for an opportunity, according to their summary mode of punishment, to throw him into the Rhone. In the year 1553, through the influence of Bertelier, the grand council of two hundred decreed that all cases of excommunication should be vested in the senate, from which body Bertelier obtained two letters of absolution. "The resolution of Calvin, however, was taken, and he was not to be daunted. He first procured the senate to be called together, stated his views and his determination, and endeavoured, but in vain, to induce them to revoke their indulgence granted to Bertelier. But receiving for answer, that "the senate changed nothing in their former decision," he, in preaching on the sunday morning previously to the administration, in a solemn tone, and with uplifted hand, uttered severe denunciations against profaners of the holy mysteries: "and for my own part," said he, "after the example of Chrysostom, I avow that I will suffer myself to be slain at the table, rather than allow this hand to deliver the sacred symbols of the Lord's body and blood to adjudged despisers of God." This was uttered with such authority, and produced such an effect, that Perrin himself immediately whispered to Bertelier that he must not present himself as a communicant. He accordingly withdrew; and the sacred ordinance, says Beza, "was celebrated with a profound silence, and under a solemn awe in all present, as if the Deity himself had been visible among them."

But there was another scene which occurred amid those factious commotions, by which Calvin was continually distressed, which deserves to be immortalized. Perrin and others having been censured by the consistory, and failing to obtain redress from the senate, appealed to the council of two hundred. Disorder, violence and sedition reigned throughout the city. On the day preceding the assembly, Calvin told his brethren that he apprehended tumult, and that it was his intention to be present. Accordingly, he and his colleagues proceeded to the council-house, where they arrived without being noticed. Before long, they heard loud and confused clamours, which were instantly increasing. The crowd heaved to and fro with all the violence of a stormy ocean chafed into ungovernable fury, and ready to overwhelm its victims in destruction. Calvin, however, like Cæsar, cast himself, alone and unprotected, into the midst of the seditious multitude. They stood aghast at his fearless presence. His friends rallied around him. Lifting his voice, he told them he came to oppose his body to their swords, and if blood was to flow, to offer his as the first sacrifice. Rushing between the parties, who were on the point of drawing their swords in mutual slaughter, he obtained a hearing; addressed them in a long and earnest oration; and so completely subdued their evil purposes, that peace, order, and tranquillity were immediately restored.

Such, by the grace of God, was the weak, timorous, and shrinking Calvin. Firm as the mountains of his country, he stood unmoved amid the storms that beat around him, and lifted his soul, undaunted, above those mists, which, to all others, shrouded the future in terrific gloom; but through which his faith, strong in the promises of God, could behold afar off the triumphs of the cause. As the twelve apostles, who fled, like frightened sheep, at the approach of danger, when endued with power from on high, were made bold as lions, so did the perfect love of Christ's truth and cause cast out all fear from the bosom of Calvin. Even in point of courage, therefore, he was not inferior to the very chiefest of reformers. But in learning, in sound and correct judgment, in prudence and moderation; in sagacity and penetration; in system and order; in cultivation and refinement of manners; in the depth and power of his intellect, Calvin shone forth amid the splendid galaxy of illustrious reformers, the star of the first magnitude and brightest lustre.

Such was the man whose life and character I now review.

## SECTION III.

#### THE GENIUS AND THE WORKS OF CALVIN.

In his early youth, Calvin manifested that genius and eloquence which characterized him as a man. The same intensity of will, the same rapidity of thought, the same retentiveness of memory, the same comprehensiveness of judgment, which enabled him to discharge the inconceivable labours of his maturer years, gave him an easy victory over all his competitors for college fame, so that it became necessary to withdraw him from the ranks, and to introduce him singly to the higher walks of learning. In his twenty-third year, he published a commentary on Seneca's treatise De Clementia, full of learning and eloquence. In his twenty-fourth year, we find him at Paris, preparing orations to be delivered by the rector of the university, and homilies to be recited to their people by the neighboring clergy. During the next year, he gave to the world his work on the sleep of the soul after death, in which he manifests an intimate acquaintance with the scriptures, and with the works of the early fathers. Thus, in the morning of his life, before others have awaked from the dreams of boyhood, or realized the responsibilities of maturer life, he was pronounced by Scaliger, who was indisposed to give praise to any, to be the most learned man in Europe. He was only in his twenty-sixth year, when he published the first edition of the Institutes of the Christian Religion, with an address to the persecuting King of France, which has ever been esteemed a production unrivalled for classic purity, force of argument, and persuasive eloquence. Designed as a defence of the calumniated reformers, and an exposure of the base injustice, tyranny, and corruption of their persecutors, this work became the bulwark of the Reformation, and the strong-hold of its adherents. It was made the confession of faith of a large portion of the protestant world, and the text book of every student. It was recommended by a convocation held at Oxford, to the general study of the English nation, and long continued to be the standard work in theology in the English universities. The Pope makes it one of his anathematizing charges against Queen Elizabeth, that the impious mysteries and institutes according to

Calvin, are received and observed by herself, and even enjoined upon all her subjects to be obeyed.* According to Schultingius, the English gave these institutes a preference to the Bible. "The Bishops," he says,† " ordered all the ministers, *ut pœne ad verbum has ediscant*—that they should learn them almost to a word;—and, *ut tum Anglice exactissime versi in singulis Ecclesiis a parochis legendi appendantur*,—that being most exactly turned into English, they should be kept in all the churches for public use;— that they were also studied in both the universities; that in Scotland the students of divinity began by reading these Institutes; that at Heidelberg, Geneva, Sorbonne, and in all the Calvinistic universities, these Institutes were publicly taught by the professors; that in Holland, ministers, civilians, and the common people, studied this work with great diligence—even the coachman and the sailor *nocturna versat manu versatque diurna;* that esteeming it as a pearl of great price, they had it bound and gilt in the most elegant manner; and that it was appealed to as a standard on all theological questions." According to this writer and the Cardinal Legate of the Pope, these Institutes were more dangerous to the cause of the papacy than all the *other* writings of the *Lutherans.*

As an author, Calvin's fame will go on brightening more and more. The Latin lan-

* Burnet's Hist. of the Reformation, vol. 2, p. 347.
† Waterman's Life, p. 137.

guage was in his day the language of the learned, and of books. But "what Latin?" asks Monsieur Villers. "A jargon bearing all the blemishes of eleven centuries of corruption and bad taste."* And yet the French Encyclopedists testify that "Calvin wrote in Latin as well as is possible in a dead language;"† and an Episcopalian of Oxford in 1839 has said, that "for majesty, when the subject required it, for purity, and in short, every quality of a perfect style, it would not suffer by a comparison with that of Cæsar, Livy or Tacitus."‡

The modern idioms also were at that time in the same uncultivated rude state in which long want of use had plunged them. Now what Luther did for the German, Calvin accomplished for the French language; he emancipated, he renovated, nay, he created it. The French of Calvin became eventually the French of Protestant France, and is still admired for its purity by the most skilful critics.§

Of his Institutes we have already spoken; "the most remarkable literary work to which the Reformation gave birth." Not less valued was his Catechism, now too much neglected and unstudied. He published it in French and Latin. It was soon translated

* Villers' Essay on the Reformation, p. 238.
† Article Geneva.
‡ Pref. to Calvin's Comment. on the Psalms, vol. 1, p. 18.
§ D'Aubigné, 3, 639, 641. French Encyclop. as above, Taylor's Biogr. of the age of Elizabeth, 2. p. 17.

into the German, English, Dutch, Scotch, Spanish, Greek, and Hebrew languages; was made one of the standards of the Church of Scotland, the basis of the early Catechism in the Church of England, and the model of the Catechism published by the Westminster Assembly of Divines.* The judgment of his great opponent, Arminius, upon Calvin's merits as a commentator, has been sustained by the verdict of three centuries, and his present advancing reputation. Arminius says, "after the holy scriptures, I exhort the students to read the commentaries of Calvin, for I tell them that he is incomparable in the interpretation of scripture, and that his commentaries ought to be held in greater estimation than all that is delivered to us in the writings of the ancient Christian fathers, so that in a certain eminent spirit of prophecy, I give the pre-eminence to him beyond most others, indeed beyond them all."† But the labours of Calvin were as multiplied and arduous as his achievements were marvellous. The Genevan edition of his works amounts to twelve folio volumes. Besides these, there exist at Geneva two thousand of his sermons and lectures taken down from his mouth as he delivered them. He was but twenty-eight years in the min-

* Waterman, 35. Waterman's edition of it, Hartford, 1815. Appendix, Irving's Confession of Faith. Pref. p. 124, and Neal's Puritans 1. 224.
† In Scott, 497. See the similar judgment of Scaliger in Bayle 265, and Beza 120, 204.

istry altogether. He was always poor, so as not to be able to have many books. The sufferings of his body from headache, weakness, and other complaints, were constant and intense, so that he was obliged to recline on his couch a part of every day. It was only the remnants of his time, left from preaching and correspondence, he devoted to study and writing. And yet, every year of his life may be chronicled by his various works. In the midst of convulsions and interruptions of every kind, he pursued his commentaries on the Bible, as if sitting in the most perfect calm, and undisturbed repose. His labours were indeed incredible and beyond all comparison. He allowed himself no recreation whatever. He preached and wrote with headaches that would, says Beza, have confined any other person to bed. He preached every day of every other week;—on Monday, Tuesday, and Wednesday, he gave lectures in theology;—on Thursday, he presided in the meeting of the presbytery;—on Friday, he expounded the holy scriptures to the congregation. His correspondence, commentaries, and controversial writings, &c., would form annually, during the period of thirty-one years, between two and three octavo volumes; and yet he never reached the age of fifty-five. When laid aside by disease from preaching, he dictated numberless letters, revised for the last time his Christian Institutes, almost re-wrote his commentary on Isaiah, frequently observing that "nothing was so painful to him as his present idle life." And when urged by his friends to forbear, he would reply, "would you have my Lord to find me idle when he cometh?"

## SECTION IV.

##### CALVIN VINDICATED FROM THE CHARGE OF AMBITION, AND HIS TRUE GREATNESS AND WONDERFUL INFLUENCE SHOWN.

Gifted with such powers of mind, and stored with such treasures of knowledge, who can question the sincerity of Calvin's adherence to the principles of the Reformation? He has been charged, however, with ambitious motives, and with aspiring to a new popedom. Shameless calumny! With the pathway to honour, emolument and fame opened to him, did he not choose, like Moses, "rather to suffer with the people of God than to enjoy the pleasures of sin for a season?" Did he not resign the benefices which he held, and which, by a covert conduct, he might still have retained, and throw himself poor and unpatronized among the houseless wanderers who were every where spoken against as not worthy to live? Did he not design to spend his time in retirement as deeming himself unfit to take part in the noble strife? Was he not led to visit Geneva by the invisible hand of God, who had obstructed his route through Dauphiny and

Savoy to Basle or Strasburgh, where he meant to retire?—Was it not after many refusals, and the extremest urgency he consented to remain in that city? And when appointed professor of divinity by the consistory and magistrates, did he not earnestly decline the office of pastor which they also insisted upon his undertaking? When banished from that place did he not again seek retirement, and with manifest reluctance resume the duties of professor and of pastor which Bucer, Capito, Hedio and the Senate of Strasburgh conferred upon him? And when the whole city of Geneva entreated his return among them, did he not say that "the further he advanced the more sensible he was how arduous a charge is that of governing a church, and that there was no place under heaven he more dreaded than Geneva." How did he praise and exalt Melancthon and Luther!* How did he bear with their opposition to his views, and their silence when he wrote to them in friendship! Did he not, when he had succeeded in founding the college at Geneva, prefer Beza to the presidency, and himself become a professor under him?† Did he not as late as 1553, in a letter to the minister of Zurich, call Farel "the father of the liberties of Geneva and the father of that church?" Ambitious! "a most extraordinary charge, says Beza, to be brought against a man who chose *his* kind

---
\* Scott's Contin. of Milner, vol. 3. 175, 414, 382, 387.
† Ibid. p. 466.

of life, and in this state, in this church, which I might truly call the very seat of poverty." No! the love of truth and of the cause of Christ, was the master passion of his soul. He realized what millions only profess, and judging with the apostle, that if Christ died for all, then were all dead, and that he thus died that they, who are made alive by his Spirit, should not henceforth live unto themselves, he consecrated his body, soul and spirit unto God. "Since," says he, "I remember that I am not my own, nor at my own disposal, I give myself up tied and bound, as a sacrifice to God." When, therefore, he was driven from Geneva by a blinded faction, amid the lamentations of his whole flock, he could say, "Had I been in the service of men, this would have been a poor reward; but it is well—I have served HIM, who never fails to repay his servants whatever he has promised." When the people of Strasburgh consented for a season to lend his service to the people of Geneva, they insisted on his retaining the privileges of a citizen and the stipend they had assigned him while resident among them. Was it ambition that led Calvin resolutely to decline the generous offer? Was it ambition which led him to settle at Geneva where his stipend, which was one hundred crowns a year, barely supported his existence, and which nevertheless he pertinaciously refused to have increased? Did he not for years abstain from all animal food at dinner, rarely eating any thing after breakfast till his stated hour for supper—and was not the whole amount of his remaining property, including his library which sold high, less than three hundred crowns? Let the infidel Bayle, who was struck with astonishment by these facts, put to silence the ignorance of foolish men.*

The charge of ambition is founded upon the innate and surpassing greatness of Calvin. An exile from his country, without money, without friends, he raised himself, by merit alone, to a dominion over the minds of men. His throne was in the hearts of those who knew him; his sceptre, truth; his laws, the silent influence of principle. Consider the difficulties which he encountered at Geneva. When he arrived in that place, in 1536, the city had neither religious nor political organization. Calvin undertook the task of giving it both.† But in order to do so, he had first to cleanse the Augean stable, to which the demoralized condition of Geneva might be well compared. The long reign of ignorance and superstition, the extreme corruption of the romish clergy, the relaxation of manners consequent upon intestine feuds and open war; the licentiousness, anarchy, and insubordination, resulting from the first excesses of unrestrained freedom, the disorders occasioned by party spirit and factious demagogues, and the secret attachment of many

* Bayle's Dict.—art. Calvin. BB. and Scott, 489.
† Dr. Taylor's Biography of the Age of Elizabeth, vol. 2. p. 24.

to the discarded system of popery—these were causes sufficient to lead to the unparalleled dissoluteness of a city, where great numbers of houses of ill fame were recognised and licensed by the magistrates, with a regular female superior, who bore the name of Reine du Bordel. Calvin proved himself to be not only a theologian of the highest order, but also a politician of astonishing sagacity. Morals became pure. The laws of the state were revised and thoroughly changed. The ecclesiastical tribunals were made independent of the civil, and a system of the strictest discipline established. The sect of the libertines was overthrown. The most powerful factions were dispersed. The enemies of truth and purity, though often triumphant, and always violent, were made to lick the dust, so that the wickedness of the wicked came to an end, and righteousness prevailed. The effects of Calvin's influence, says a recent and prejudiced historian, "after the lapse of ages, are still visible in the industry and intellectual tone of Geneva."* From having been a small and unimportant town, Geneva became the focus of light, the centre of attraction, and the source of incalculable influence upon the destinies of Europe and the world. Calvin's seminary supplied teachers and ministers to most of the reformed states of Europe. Geneva was honoured with the title of the mother of pro-

* Hist. of Switzerland. Lond., 1832; p. 227.

testantism. Lodgings could with difficulty be found for the multitude of students that came to sit at the feet of the man whom Melancthon called "the divine." It was to this "metropolis of presbyterianism" all the proscribed exiles who were driven from other countries by the intolerance of popery, "came to get intoxicated with presbytery and republicanism," to carry back with them those seeds which have sprung up in the republic of Holland, the commonwealth of England, the glorious revolution of 1688, and our own American confederation.

Would you see the amazing power and influence of Calvin, read the history of his triumph over Bolsec, one of those hydras of faction that successively shot up their revegetating heads in Geneva.* Behold Troillet, another of his enemies, when about to die, sending for Calvin that he might confess his faults, declaring that he could not die in peace without obtaining his forgiveness. Behold him at Berne, debating against Castalio and others with such power that his opponents were henceforth excluded from that Canton. Thus, like another Hercules, armed with the simple club of God's holy word, did he destroy the numerous monsters who threatened to overthrow the truth as it is in Jesus.

How wonderful was the influence, under God, of this single man! The reformed

* Scott ibid. 404, and Waterman 70.

churches in France adopted his confession of faith, and were modeled after the ecclesiastical order of Geneva. To him England is indebted for her articles, for a purified liturgy, and for all her psalmody.* To him Scotland owes her Knox, her Buchanan, and her Melville, her ecclesiastical system, and all that has made her proudly eminent among the nations of the earth. To him, Northern Ireland is indebted for the industry, manufactures, education, religion, and noble spirit of independence and freedom which she received from her first settlers, the followers of Calvin.† To his letters, dedications, and exhortations every nation of any eminence in his day, was accustomed to pay profound respect. These writings had a salutary influence even upon the romish church. Her shame was excited, abuses were abandoned, discipline enforced, and the necessity of a reformation confessed. Nor was this influence merely ecclesiastical or political. The increase of his own church was, we are told, wonderful, and he could say, even during his life, "I have numberless spiritual children throughout the world." His contemporaneous reputation was even greater than his posthumous fame, because all parties united in rendering him honour. Many romanists, says Bayle, "would do him justice if they

* Sibson in Beza's Life, Am. ed.; p. 111, 112.
† Waterman, p. 34. Scott ibid. 370. Beza's Life, p. 101.

durst." Scaliger said he was "the greatest wit the world had seen since the Apostles," while the romish bishop of Valence called him "the greatest divine in the world."* The romanists too have been forced to acknowledge the falsity of their infamous calumnies published against his morals.† Such was the terror he had inspired in this great apostasy, that when a false report of his death was circulated they decreed a public procession, and returned thanks to God in their churches for his death.‡ Every pious, eminent, and learned reformer was his friend. It was the power of his reputation, proclaiming abroad their own condemnation, that led the General Assembly of Geneva to adopt a decree for his return,—to acknowledge the great injury they had done him, and implore forgiveness of Almighty God,—to send an honourable deputation to him to persuade him to accept—to go forth in throngs to welcome his return—and to allow him a secretary at the public expense. In short, it would be no difficult matter, as has been said, to prove, that there is not a parallel instance upon record, of any single individual being equally and so unequivocally venerated, for the union of wisdom and piety, both in England, and by a large body of the foreign churches, as John Calvin.

* Bayle's Dict. Fol. 2. p. 268; note X.
† Ibid, p. 265, and note 2.
‡ Waterman, p. 135.

## SECTION V.

CALVIN VINDICATED FROM THE CHARGE OF ILLIBERALITY, INTOLERANCE, AND PERSECUTION.

But we will pass on to another view of Calvin's character. A truly great mind, conscious of its own resources, and more fully sensible than others of the difficulties surrounding every subject of human speculation, is always calm and tempered with moderation, equally free from bigotry and indifference. It has therefore been attempted to deprive Calvin of his glory, by the allegation that he was illiberal, extravagant, and intolerant,—a furious bigot and extreme ultraist,—and the most heartless of persecutors. Such charges, in such an age and country as this, are, it is well known, the most offensive, and the most sure to cover with obloquy, the man, and the cause with which he is identified. But the very reverse we affirm to be the truth in the case. Calvin was liberal in his views, moderate in his spirit, and tolerant in his disposition.

Who had endured greater calumny, reproach, and hatred, at the hands of the romanists, than Calvin? and yet he allowed the validity of romish baptism, and the claims of Rome to the character of a church, not merely as comprising many of God's elect children, but as having "the remains of a church continuing with them."* Against whom did Luther and his coadjutors utter severer language, than against Calvin in reference to the sacramentarian controversy? And whom did Calvin more delight to honor than Luther? How did he study to cover the coals of this pernicious discord, and if possible, entirely to quench them? "I wish you," he says, writing to Bullinger and the other pastors of Zurich, against whom Luther had used an inexcusable wantonness of language, reproach, and anathema, " I wish you to recall these things to your mind: how great a man Luther is, and with how great gifts he excels; also with what fortitude and constancy of mind, with what efficacy of learning, he hath hitherto laboured and watched to destroy the kingdom of antichrist, and to propagate, at the same time, the doctrine of salvation. I often say, if he should call me a devil, I hold him in such honour, that I would acknowledge him an eminent servant of God." And does not the whole protestant world now, including the Lutheran church itself, acknowledge that the doctrine of Calvin on the Lord's Supper is true, scriptural, and catholic, and that Luther's was as certainly extravagant and wrong?

In how many ways did he endeavour

---

* "However broken and deformed it may be, a church of some sort exists," and in proof of this, he quotes 2 Thess. ii. 4. See his letters to Socinus in 1549, and Scott ibid. 400.

to preserve the peace and harmony of the churches; to lead to compromise on matters of order and discipline; to encourage submission to ceremonies and forms which were in themselves "fooleries," rather than produce rupture and give occasion to the enemy to blaspheme; to prevent schism, disunion, and alienation, and to bind together with the cords of love the whole brotherhood of the reformed churches! "Keep your smaller differences," says he, addressing the Lutheran churches, "let us have no discord on that account; but let us march in one solid column, under the banners of the captain of our salvation, and with undivided counsels pour the legions of the cross upon the territories of darkness and of death." "I should not hesitate to cross ten seas, if by this means holy communion might prevail among the members of Christ."

Nothing can be more liberal than his views as to the character of other churches. "Let the ministers," he says,* "therefore, by whom God permits the church to be governed, be what they may, if the signs of the true church are perceived, it will be better not to separate from their communion. Nor is it an objection, that some impure doctrines are there delivered; for there is scarce any church which retains none of the remains of ignorance. It is sufficient for us, that the doctrine, on which the church of Christ is

* Letter to Farel from Strasburgh, 1538, in Waterman, p. 249, 250.

founded, should hold its place and influence."
Hence has it happened that the most absurd
attempts have been made, even in our own
day, to represent Calvin as the friend and
defender of prelacy which he spent his life
in opposing—that liberality which made him
willing to bear, for a time, with the "tolerable fooleries" of the ritual of the English
church, being most ungenerously and falsely
interpreted into a warm and hearty approval
of its unscriptural forms which Calvin openly
and constantly condemned.*

Equally liberal and moderate was Calvin
in his doctrinal tenets. He steered the safe
and middle course between antinomianism
and arminianism—and between fatalism and
latitudinarianism. No one has ever been
more belied. Garbled extracts have been
made to give expression to views which their
context was designed to overthrow. Doctrines have been fathered upon Calvin which
had existed in the church from the Apostles'
days, and in every age. And erroneous opinions both doctrinal and practical, have been
attributed to him which he spent his life in
opposing, and of which no confutation could
be found more triumphant than what is given
in his own works. But while these are
unknown or unread, youthful bigots, and
learned fools, expose their shame by retailing

* See Calvin's views on the subject of Episcopacy, fully vindicated and established, by Dr. Miller, in his recent letters to Bishop Ives, and also in his work on the Christian Ministry, 2d ed. 8vo.

and perpetuating stereotyped abuse. It were enough to repel all such criminations by the fact that for every doctrine Calvin appeals to the Bible—that he exalts the Bible above every human authority, including his own—that he claims for all men liberty of conscience and of judgment—and leaves them to search the Scriptures that they may thus try his doctrines whether they be of God.

In particular, the doctrines of predestination, decrees, and divine sovereignty, were not peculiar to Calvin, but were common to him with the greatest divines of all ages, and with all the reformers. He was, too, a sub- and not a supra-lapsarian. He does not represent God as arbitrary. He utterly repudiates, and constantly opposes, fatalism.* He always inculcates the duty and necessity of using means; condemning the confounding of "necessity with compulsion," and rejecting the supposition as absurd, that "man's being actuated by God is incompatible with his being at the same time active himself."† He teaches that these means of grace, such as exhortations, precepts, and reproofs, are not confined to those who are already pious, but are God's means of awakening the careless, converting the sinner, and leaving the impenitent without excuse. He teaches, therefore, that sinners are constantly to be urged to attendance upon God's ordinances, and to the diligent and prayerful use of all the means by which they may be convinced,

* Institutes, B. I., ch. xvi. § 8, 9.
† Ibid. B. II., ch. iii. § 5, and B. I. ch. xviii. § 2.

converted, and saved.* He strenuously upholds the free agency and responsibility of man.† He rejects the doctrine of reprobation, as it is vulgarly believed, since he attributes the final condemnation of the wicked to themselves, and not to any arbitrary decree of God.‡

While Calvin held firmly to the great fundamental doctrine of imputation, and to the doctrine of a limited atonement, he nevertheless rejected all such views of the sacrifice of Christ as would make him to have suffered just so much for each one that was to be saved by him, so that if more or fewer had been appointed unto salvation, he must have shed accordingly more or fewer drops of his

---

\* Instit. B. II. ch. v. § 1, 4, 5, &c.

† See numerous extracts in proof in Scott's Contin. of Milner, vol. ii. pp. 508, 521, 525, 379, 385, 405.

‡ Instit., B. III., ch. xxiv., is entitled "Election Confirmed (i. e., made surely known to us. Scott ibid. p. 577) by the divine calling, the just destruction to which the reprobate are destined, *procured by themselves.*" In the epistle of the pastors of Geneva, (Calv. Epist. p. 63–65, in Scott 406,) we find reprobation most offensively spoken of as proceeding "from the bare will and pleasure of God"—nudo Dei placito—when no such thing as we should understand by the words is meant. This appears from what presently follows: "It is beyond controversy, that the perdition of men is to be ascribed to their own wickedness;" and that the punishments which God inflicts on them are "deserved." It would seem that all which they mean, and which Calvin generally, at least, means by such obnoxious language, is, that among a *fallen* and *guilty* race, God, according to his sovereign pleasure, chooses whom he will to bring to salvation, and whom (according to the title of Calvin's work on Predestination) he will "leave in their ruin." This appears to be the constant meaning of Calvin, in the work which he now published on these subjects.

precious blood, and suffered more or less severe dying pangs. Calvin on the contrary, recognized in the death of Christ, a sacrifice adequate to the sins of the whole world, and which made provision for all whom it should please the Father to enable and dispose to avail themselves of it.*

He therefore fully and frequently proclaims the universality of the gospel promises, and the duty of all to receive and embrace them.† While he teaches that original sin is natural, he denies that it originated from nature. "We deny," says he, "that it proceeded from nature, to signify that it is rather an adventitious quality or accident, than a substantial property, originally innate, yet we call it natural, that no one may suppose it to be contracted by every individual from corrupt habit, whereas it prevails over all by hereditary right." "No other explanation therefore

---

* On Romans v. 18,—"The free gift came on all men to justification of life," he remarks, "The apostle makes it a grace or favour common to all, because it is proposed (or set forth) to all; not because it is actually extended to (conferred on) all. For, though Christ suffered for the sins of the whole world, and is offered by the mercy of God to all indifferently, (without exception or distinction,) yet all do not embrace him." On 1 John ii. 2, he says: "Christ suffered sufficiently for the whole world, but efficaciously only for the elect." And finally, as early as the year 1535, in a preface to the New Testament in French, he says: "At the appointed time the Messiah came, and amply performed whatever was necessary for the redemption of all. The benefit was not confined to Israel alone: it was rather to be extended to the whole human race; because by Christ alone the whole human race was to be reconciled to God."

† Instit. B. III. ch. iii., § 21, and ch. xxii; § 10, and ch. xxiv. § 6, 8, 16, 17, and Scott, p. 597.

can be given of our being said to be dead in Adam, than that his transgression not only procured misery and ruin for himself, but also precipitated our nature into similar destruction, and that not by his personal guilt as an individual, which pertains not to us, but because he infected all his descendants with the corruption into which he had fallen." And again—"We are, on account of this very corruption, considered as convicted and justly condemned in the sight of God, to whom nothing is acceptable but righteousness, innocence, and purity. And this liability to punishment arises not from the delinquency of another, for when it is said that the sin of Adam renders us obnoxious to the divine judgment, it is not to be understood as if we, though innocent, were undeservedly loaded with the guilt of his sin, but because we are all subject to a curse, in consequence of his transgression, he is therefore said to have involved us in guilt. Nevertheless we derive from him not only the punishment, but also the pollution to which the punishment is justly due."*

He allows that even as fallen, "the soul of man is irradiated with a beam of divine light, so that it is never wholly destitute of some little flame or at least spark of it," though "it cannot comprehend God by that illumination," the remaining image of God being but the ruin of the original, and "confused, mutilated, and defiled."†

* Instit. B. II. ch. i. § 10, 11, and B. II., ch. 1, § 6, 8.
† Ibid. B. I., ch. xv., § 4 & 6; B. II., ch. ii., § 12, and B. II., ch. 1, § 13, 19, 22, 24, and ch. iii., § 4.

His doctrines, therefore, as he frequently shows, cut up by the roots all presumption, prevent despair, encourage hope, and in an eminent degree enforce and cherish holiness both of heart and life.* His doctrines also make special provision for the salvation of all elect children whether baptized or unbaptized, whether christian or pagan; nor did he ever discountenance the idea that all children dying in infancy may be regarded as among the elect, and therefore as assuredly saved.† He also approved the baptism of the infants of all baptized parents whether communicants or not, recognizing the covenant right of such children to the seal of those privileges to which they have a natural and necessary claim.

I may also mention, as interesting at this time, that Calvin approved of a public form for the introduction of professors into the Christian church.‡

Now let these views of Calvin be com-

* Ibid. B. III., ch. xxiv. § 4, and ch. xiv. § 17—21.
† In his Instit. B. IV., ch. xvi., where he argues against those who affirmed that regeneration cannot take place in early infancy—"God," says he, "adopts infants and washes them in the blood of his Son," and "they are regarded by Christ as among his flock." Again, (Instit. B. IV., ch. xvi., § 31, p. 461, see also p. 435, 436, 451,) he says of John iii. 36, "Christ is not speaking of the general guilt in which all the descendants of Adam are involved, but only threatening the despisers of the gospel who proudly and obstinately reject the grace that is offered them; and this has nothing to do with infants. I likewise oppose a contrary argument; all those whom Christ blesses are exempted from the curse of Adam and the wrath of God; and it is known that infants were blessed by him; it follows that they are exempted from death."
‡ Ibid. B. IV., ch. xix. § 4, 13.

pared with those of Luther and Melancthon on the subject of predestination, or with those of Beza, his own coadjutor; or with those of the English Reformers and the Lambeth articles; and will they not be allowed, by every impartial judge, to be at once liberal, moderate and wise. While these doctrines, by which alone many know Calvin, were not peculiar to him, it is also true that they were not dwelt upon with any undue prominence, but in subordination to other subjects. And when the unparalleled consistency with which through his whole life Calvin continued to maintain the same views, is contrasted with the variation of others, how illustriously do they exhibit the superiority of his intellectual powers. Not that he was infallible—far from it. He too was human, fallible, and chargeable with error. In making assurance of salvation necessary to a true faith—in questioning the peculiar and permanent sanctity of the Sabbath day—in supposing that Christ descended to hell, or endured on the cross the torments of hell— Calvin certainly erred, and is not by any to be believed or followed.\*

But we proceed to remark that Calvin was not intolerant in spirit or in practice. It is true, that Servetus was, at his prosecution, brought to trial for conduct the most criminal and opinions the most horrible, which in the face of the laws and of repeated admonition he continued to propagate with pestiferous

\* See Scott's Contin. of Milner, vol. 3, p. 545, 550, and 583, and Bib. Repertory, 1831, p. 421.

zeal. But that Calvin did more than this, in the whole course of his life, to give occasion to the charges of persecuting intolerance so loudly proclaimed against him, we positively deny. To affirm, as many do, that he sought the burning of Servetus—that he influenced the Senate in securing his death— that he aided or abetted in his execution— or that he did not use his best endeavours to procure a mitigation of his sentence—is an atrocious calumny against the truth of history, and an act of black persecution against the memory of a great and good man. We have already offered proof of the liberality and moderation of Calvin even towards opponents. Many similar facts illustrative of his great forbearance might be adduced. His benevolence no one can dispute. Nor can any one question his humble and unambitious spirit. The earlier editions of his Institutes contained also the following eloquent argument in favour of toleration. "Though it may be wrong to form friendship or intimacy with those who hold pernicious opinions, yet must we contend against them only by exhortation, by kindly instructions, by clemency, by mildness, by prayers to God, that they may be so changed as to bear good fruits, and be restored to the unity of the church. And not only are erring Christians to be so treated, but even Turks and Saracens."*

This, then, was the natural spirit, and the genuine creed of Calvin. But it was dia-

* Dr. Taylor's Biography of the Age of Elizabeth, vol. 2, p. 46.

metrically opposed to the spirit and to the universal sentiment of the age. The Romish church had diffused the notion that the spirit of the judicial laws of the Old Testament still constituted the rule and standard of the Christian church. Of necessity, therefore, a regard for the public peace, and the preservation of the church of Christ from infection, required the punishment of heretics and blasphemers.* Toleration of errorists was deemed sinful, and their destruction a Christian duty. Men were taught to believe that temporal penalties were God's appointed means for making men virtuous and religious. The gibbet, the stake, the cell, and various other modes of torture, were therefore the chief arguments employed. Priests became inquisitors. The pulpit was the inciter to slaughter: and *Te Deums* resounded through cloistered walls in commemoration of the deaths of infamous heretics. Persecution, in short, was the avowed policy of the church. Now the Reformers, be it remembered, were all Romish theologians, trained up in the bosom of the Roman church, and imbued with these fatal sentiments, which were every where applauded.†

The liberty of the Reformation, also, had been abused to the greatest licentiousness, both of opinion and of practice. Such heresies in doctrine, and excesses in conduct, were all employed as arguments against the Reformers. While, then, tolerance of error was a standing reproach in the mouth of Rome,

* See Clarke's Hist. of Intol., vol. 1. p. xviii. and xxi.
† Viller on the Reformation, p. 260.

against their cause, the reformers, deluded in their first principles—blinded by the universal opinion of all parties—and driven, in self-defence, to oppose themselves to all heresy—continued to approve and to practise upon those views which are now condemned as intolerance and persecution. Calvin, therefore, was led to think that his previous views would encourage heresy, and injure the cause of the reform; and for once, he allowed his better judgment to be warped, and fully endorsed the principle that heresy must be restrained by force. But still he utterly disclaimed all right or power to employ that force on the part of the church. He transferred it altogether to the civil authorities, and therefore to the hands of the community, generally, by whom it has been ultimately abolished. Tried, therefore, by the universal judgment of his age, Calvin was not intolerant; and when condemned by the free and liberal views of the present time, he meets his sentence in common with all men, whether civilians or theologians, and with all the reformers, whether continental or anglican.* So that the whole guilt of the persecuting tenets of the reformers must ultimately rest upon that mother from whose breasts these all had drawn the milk of intolerance, and by whose nurture they had been trained up in the way of persecution.

* Scott's Contin., vol. 3, 420, 432, 433, 435, 437, 438, D'Aubigné Hist. of Ref., vol. 3, p. 630. Beza's Life, p. 109, 110, 156, 197.

The romish church, therefore, as has been truly said, is answerable for the execution of Servetus.

If, however, there ever was a case in which the execution of the penalty of death could have been properly inflicted, it was in that of Servetus. Never had man so blasphemed his Maker, so outraged christian feeling and all propriety, so insulted the laws in force for his destruction, and so provoked the slumbering arm of vengeance to fall upon him.[*]

Servetus had been driven from every attempted residence on account of his unbearable conduct. He had been tried and condemned to be burned to death by the romanists at Vienna, from whose hands he had just escaped when he came to Geneva.[†] He was well aware of the intolerant character of the laws of the city of Geneva, enacted against heretics by the Emperor Frederick I. when under imperial and romish jurisdiction—which had been often exercised before that time—and which were still in force.[‡] Calvin, regarding his sentiments and conduct with just abhorrence, and believing it to be his duty, for the reasons stated, to oppose them, gave him previous notice, that if he came to the city of Geneva, he should be under the necessity of prosecuting him. There was, therefore, no previous

---

[*] Beza's Life, p. 163, 203. Philad. ed.
[†] Scott ibid. 423, Beza ibid. 163.
[‡] Scott ibid. 347, 356, 374, 430, 443. Beza ibid. 167, 180, and 199.

malice in Calvin towards him. When Servetus had come, and Calvin had brought his character and opinions to the view of the authorities, his interference in the matter there ceased. He never visited the court, except when required to do so. The Senate, instead of being influenced by him in the course they pursued, were, the greater part of them, at that very time opposed to him.* The whole matter was, at Servetus' request, submitted to the judgment of the other cities, who unanimously approved of his condemnation.†

Servetus, too, acknowledged the justice of his own sentence, if guilty of the charges made against him,—and which were all sustained,—and actually sought and hoped to have the same sentence inflicted upon Calvin.‡ He therefore forced death upon himself, and threw himself, as it were, into the burning fire; Calvin having exerted his utmost influence, up to the very last, to have the mode of execution altered.

Now when it is remembered that at this very time the flames were consuming the victims of romish persecution, and also those of Cranmer, who is called a pattern of humility—that Davides fell a victim to the intolerance of Socinus§—that the English reformers applauded the execution of Servetus —that his punishment was regarded as the

* Scott ibid., p. 434, 440. Beza's Life ibid. 168, 283.
† Scott ibid. 427, 436. Beza's Life ibid. 169, 195.
‡ Waterman's Life of Calvin, p. 103, 105.
§ Scott, ibid. 439. Williams' Relig. Liberty, p. 135.

common cause of all the churches—and that for fifty years no writer criminated Calvin for his agency in this matter—may we not say to those who now try Calvin by an *ex post facto* law—let him that is guiltless among you cast the first stone? So much for the charge of intolerance.

## SECTION VI.

##### CALVIN VINDICATED FROM THE CHARGE OF A WANT OF NATURAL AFFECTION AND FRIENDSHIP.

Equally futile and untrue is another charge made against Calvin, that he was entirely destitute of tenderness and all natural affection, and that no expression of kindness can be found in his writings. That his intellectual powers were pre-eminent, and held his passions, appetites and desires in complete subjection to the dictates of prudence and calm sobriety, is unquestionably true. But that Calvin possessed deep feeling, and was susceptible of the strongest and most tender emotions, we believe to be incontrovertibly certain. "I had intended," he says, on his return to the people of Geneva, who had so cruelly treated him, "to address the people, entering into a review of the past, and a justification of myself and my colleagues; but I found them so touched with remorse, so ready to anticipate me in the confession of their faults, that I felt that such a proceeding would not only be superfluous but cruel." . "It was beautiful," says Beza, " to observe the union of these three great men—i. e., Calvin, Farel and Viret— in the service of their common Master." When Farel wished to visit him in his last illness, Calvin wrote him, saying—" Farewell, my best and most worthy brother. Since God has determined that you should survive me in this world, live mindful of our union, which has been so useful to the church of God, and the fruits of which await us in heaven. Do not fatigue yourself on my account. I draw my breath with difficulty, and am expecting continually that my breath will fail. It is sufficient that I live and die in Christ, who is gain to his servants in life and in death. Again, farewell with the brethren."

After the death of his friend Courault, he says, in a letter to Farel, "I am so overwhelmed, that I put no limits to my sorrow. My daily occupations have no power to retain my mind from recurring to the event, and revolving constantly the impressive thought. The distressing impulses of the day are followed by the more torturing anguish of the night. I am not only troubled with dreams, to which I am inured by habit, but I am greatly enfeebled by the restless watchings which are extremely injurious to my health."

On the death of Bucer, he thus writes:—

"I feel my heart to be almost torn asunder, when I reflect on the very great loss which the church has sustained in the death of Bucer, and on the advantages that England would have derived from his labours, had he been spared to assist in carrying on the reformation in that kingdom."

Look, also, at his letters of consolation, addressed to those confessors for the truth who had been unable to make their escape from persecution.*

On the death of his son, he wrote to Viret, saying, "The Lord hath certainly inflicted a heavy and severe wound on us, by the death of our little son; but He is our father, and knows what is expedient for his children." And when his wife was taken from him, we behold in Calvin all the tenderness of a most sensitive and affectionate heart. Writing to Farel, to whom he gives a detail of her illness, he says: "The report of the death of my wife has doubtless reached you before this. I use every exertion in my power not to be entirely overcome with heaviness of heart. My friends, who are about me, omit nothing that can afford alleviation to the depression of my mind." Again, "may the Lord Jesus strengthen you by his Spirit, and me also in this so great calamity, which would inevitably have overpowered me, unless from heaven he stretched forth his hand, whose office it is to raise the fallen,

* Scott's Contin. of Milner, p. 374.

to strengthen the weak, and to refresh the weary." Again writing to Viret, he says, "although the death of my wife is a very severe affliction, yet I repress as much as I am able, the sorrow of my heart. My friends also afford every anxious assistance, yet with all our exertions, we effect less, in assuaging my grief, than I could wish; but still the consolation which I obtain I cannot express. You know the tenderness of my mind, or rather with what effeminacy I yield under trials; so that without the exercise of much moderation, I could not have supported the pressure of my sorrow. Certainly it is no common occasion of grief. I am deprived of a most amiable partner, who, whatever might have occurred of extreme endurance, would have been my willing companion, not only in exile and poverty, but even in death. While she lived, she was indeed the faithful helper of my ministry, and on no occasion did I ever experience from her any interruption. For your friendly consolation, I return you my sincere thanks. Farewell, my dear and faithful brother. May the Lord Jesus watch over and direct you and your wife. To her and the brethren express my best salutation."

Now, if these proofs of the tenderness of Calvin are not sufficient, let any one read the account of his closing scenes, and he will find the most touching manifestations of an affectionate and tender spirit. As a brother, friend, husband, father, and minister, Calvin displayed warm, steady, and unshaken friendship and regard.

---

## SECTION VII.

#### THE OBLIGATIONS WHICH WE OWE TO CALVIN AS AMERICAN CITIZENS AND CHRISTIANS, ILLUSTRATED.

Such was Calvin, and such the triumphant defence of his character against all assaults, which he has left behind him in his unspotted life, his unimpeachable character, his familiar epistles, and his everlasting works. His wisdom, learning, prudence, and unapproachable excellencies as an author, no one has ever dared to dispute. The star of his fame has continued to shine with ever-increasing brilliancy in the intellectual firmament, and still guides many a voyager over the dark and uncertain sea of time to the sure haven of everlasting blessedness. Such is the rich inheritance he left us, who would desire to be followers of him as far as he followed Christ. But this is not all. To him we are indebted for other treasures, dearly prized by every American citizen.

We look, for instance, to our system of common schools as the great hope of American freedom, in the intelligence they every where diffuse. Now, Calvin was the father of popular education, and the inventor of the system of free schools. None of the reformers perceived more clearly the advantages of education, or laboured more earnestly to promote it. Next to our common schools, we prize our colleges and theological seminaries as the nurseries of citizens, statesmen, and ministers, capable of guarding the affairs of a great and free people. Now the building and complete endowment of the college and seminary at Geneva, was among the last acts accomplished by Calvin—it having been opened in 1559, with 600 students. "Even now, when Geneva has generally deserted the standards of the original reformers, and joined those of Arius and Socinus, her sons rejoice in the great triumph achieved by the wisdom of Calvin over the power of Napoleon, who, on conquering Geneva, wanted courage to make any change in the system of education, which had been planted more than 200 years before Bonaparte was born, by this distinguished friend of genuine Christianity, and a truly scriptural education."

We hail the birth-day of our country's liberty. We still commemorate the declaration of our national independence. We glory in a country more rapidly extending its territory, its population, and its riches, than any other upon earth—in laws the most just and impartial—in a government the most equitable, economical and free—and in the enjoyment of a religious liberty more perfect and complete than can be paralleled in the history of man. The star spangled banner awakens the envy and the admiration of the world—and our glorious republic is the fairy vision which excites the emulous desire of imitation in the bosom of every well-wisher to the advancement of society. But whence came all these? "The pilgrims of Plymouth," says Bancroft, "were Calvinists; the best influence in South Carolina came from the Calvinists of France; William Penn was the disciple of the Huguenots; the ships from Holland that first brought colonists to Manhattan, were filled with Calvinists. He that will not honour the memory and respect the influence of Calvin, knows but little of the origin of American liberty." Yes! Calvin was a thorough-going republican. The Institutes of Calvin carry with the truths of Christianity the seeds of republicanism to the ends of the earth. "Indeed," says he,* "if these three forms of government, which are stated by philosophers, be considered in themselves, I shall by no means deny, that either aristocracy, or a mixture of aristocracy and democracy, far excels all others; and that, indeed, not of itself, but because it very rarely happens, that kings regulate themselves, so that their will is never at variance with justice and rectitude; or in the next place, that they are endued with such penetration and prudence, as in all cases to discover what is best. The vice or imperfection of men, therefore, renders it safer and

* Inst. B. IV. c. 20. § 8.

more tolerable for the government to be in hands of many, that they may afford each other mutual assistance and admonition, and that if any one arrogate to himself more than is right, the many may act as censors, and masters, to restrain his ambition. / This has always been proved by experience, and the Lord confirmed it by his authority, when he established a government of this kind among the people of Israel, with a view to preserve them in the most desirable condition, till he exhibited, in David, a type of Christ. And as I readily acknowledge, that no kind of government is more happy than this, where liberty is regulated with becoming moderation, and properly established on a durable basis, so also I consider these as the most happy people, who are permitted to enjoy such a condition; and if they exert their strenuous and constant efforts for its preservation, I admit that they act in perfect consistence with their duty."

"Calvin," says Bishop Horsley, "was unquestionably, in theory, a republican; he freely declares his opinion, that the republican form, or an aristocracy reduced nearly to the level of a republic, was of all the best calculated, in general, to answer the ends of government. So wedded, indeed, was he to this notion, that, in disregard of an apostolic institution, and the example of the primitive ages, he endeavored to fashion the government of all the protestant churches upon republican principles; and his persevering zeal in that attempt, though in this country, through the mercy of God, it failed, was followed, upon the whole, with a wide and mischievous success. But in civil politics, though a republican in theory, he was no leveller."

Geneva, the mother of modern republics, is the monument of Calvin's fame; and as Montesquieu says, should celebrate, in annual festival, the day when Calvin first entered that city. Politically and ecclesiastically, Calvin honoured the people; assumed their intelligence, virtue, and worth; and entrusted them with the management of affairs. He taught, also, the spiritual independence of the church; its entire separation from civil government; and the supreme and exclusive headship of its only lawgiver and sovereign, the Lord Jesus Christ. These were the grand truths taught and illustrated by Calvin; truths which drew the lovers of freedom to Geneva, which sent them away burning with the thirst for liberty and republicanism, which aroused the slumbering people of Europe, which convulsed France, confederated the states of Holland, revolutionized England, Presbyterianized Scotland, colonized New England, and founded this great and growing republic.*

* "He lived in a day when nations were shaken to their centre, by the excitement of the Reformation, when the fields of Holland and France were wet with the carnage of persecution; when vindictive monarchs on the one side threatened all Protestants with outlawry and death, and the Vatican on the other sent forth its anathemas and

This, too, is an age of missions. The missionary enterprise is the glory of the church, the regenerator of society, the precursor of the millennial reign of peace and happiness, and the hope of the world. With generous emulation, all branches of the church catholic strive for the mastery in this glorious achievement, while Ichabod is written upon any denomination from whose battlements the gospel banner is not unfurled, and whose laggard troops come not up to the help of the Lord, to the help of the Lord against the mighty. Now it was Calvin who led on this mighty enterprise, and gave birth to this modern crusade against the powers of darkness. He alone, so far as we know, of all the reformers, while battling with surrounding foes, remembered the waste places

its cry for blood. In that day, it is too true, the influence of an ancient, long-established, hardly disputed error, the constant danger of his position, the intensest desire to secure union among the antagonists of popery, the engrossing consciousness that this struggle was for the emancipation of the Christian world, induced the great reformer to defend the use of the sword for the extirpation of error. Reprobating and lamenting his adhesion to the cruel doctrine, which all christendom had for centuries implicitly received, we may, as republicans, remember that Calvin was not only the founder of a sect, but foremost among the most efficient of modern republican legislators. More truly benevolent to the human race than Solon, more self-denying than Lycurgus, the genius of Calvin infused enduring elements into the institutions of Geneva, and made it for the modern world the impregnable fortress of popular liberty, the fertile seed-plot of democracy.—*From an Address to the public, by G. Bancroft, Esq.*

of the earth which are full of the habitations of horrid cruelty, and connected his name with the very earliest attempt to establish a Protestant mission in the heathen world. He united with the admiral de Coligny in establishing a colony on the coast of Brazil, to which he sent Peter Richter and several others from Geneva, who were accompanied with numerous French Protestants.* Presbytery and missions are therefore coeval, co-extensive, and inseparable. They went hand in hand during the first six centuries. They again clasped hands in indissoluble union at the era of the Reformation. They have lived together in wedded peace, harmony and zeal. And whom God hath so joined together, let no apathy, or unbelief, or opinions, ever put asunder.

To bequeath to us, his spiritual descendants, these incomparable blessings, Calvin early sacrificed the glittering crown of academic fame, and certain worldly aggrandisement and honour,—became an exile from home, kindred and country,—endured calumny, reproach, persecution, banishment and poverty, wore out his weak and suffering body with excessive and unremitting toil,—and at the early age of 54 sunk into the tomb.†

* Scott, ibid. p. 462. 464.
† There is another blessing for which, as Christians, we are indebted to Calvin, and which cannot be too highly estimated; I mean congregational psalmody. Calvin encouraged Marot to make his metrical version of the Psalms.

## SECTION VIII.

#### THE CLOSING SCENES OF CALVIN'S LIFE.

LET us, then, before we take our leave, draw near, and contemplate the last act in the drama of this great and good man's life.

He wrote a preface to them, when first published, in 1543. He took care to have them set to music by the most distinguished musicians. He then introduced them into the public service of the church. The mode of singing psalms in measured verse was thus first introduced by Calvin, at Geneva, in 1543. From that church the practice went forth into all the reformed churches in France, and was introduced into England by the Presbyterians who resided at Geneva, and established an English church there during the *Marian persecution*. The English exiles, while at Geneva, commenced and completed a translation of the Scriptures into the English language. The principal translators were Miles Coverdale, Christopher Goodman, John Knox, Anthony Gilby, or Gibbs, Thomas Sampson, William Cole, and William Whittingham. They divided the chapters into verses, and added notes in the margin, and also tables, maps, &c., and published it, with a dedication to Queen Elizabeth, in 1560. The psalms, versified and set to music, as in the church of Geneva, were annexed to this Bible. This version has been known as that of Sternhold and Hopkins. The initials of the name of the versifier were prefixed to each psalm. Thus the psalms, versified in English, came into England, and were allowed, first, to be sung before the morning and evening service; and at length they were published with this declaration:—*Psalms set forth and allowed to be sung in all churches, before and after morning and evening prayer, as also before and after sermons.* And in a short time they superseded the *Te Deum, Benedicte, Magnificat,* and *Nunc dimittis,* which had been retained from the Romish church. Bayle, Art. Marot; Neal, p. 109; Heylin, p. 213, 214; Rees' Cy., art. Bible; Burnet, p. 290; Waterman's Life of Calvin, p. 403.

Methinks I see that emaciated frame, that sunken cheek, and that bright, ethereal eye, as Calvin lay upon his study-couch. He heeds not the agonies of his frame, his vigorous mind rising in its power as the outward man perished in decay. The nearer he approached his end, the more energetically did he ply his unremitted studies. In his severest pains he would raise his eyes to heaven and say, How long, O Lord! and then resume his efforts. When urged to allow himself repose, he would say, "What! would you that when the Lord comes he should surprise me in idleness?" Some of his most important and laboured commentaries were therefore finished during this last year.

On the 10th of March, his brother ministers coming to him, with a kind and cheerful countenance he warmly thanked them for all their kindness, and hoped to meet them at their regular assembly for the last time, when he thought the Lord would probably take him to himself. On the 27th, he caused himself to be carried to the senate-house, and being supported by his friends, he walked into the hall, when, uncovering his head, he returned thanks for all the kindness they had shown him, especially during his sickness. With a faltering voice, he then added, "I think I have entered this house for the last time," and, mid flowing tears, took his leave. On the 2d of April, he was carried to the church, where he received the sacrament at the hands of Beza, joining in the hymn with such an expression of joy in his countenance, as attracted the notice of the congregation. Having made his will on the 27th of this month,* he sent to inform the syndics and the members of the senate that he desired once more to address them in their hall, whither he wished to be carried the next day. They sent him word that they would wait on him, which they accordingly did, the next day, coming to him from the senate-house. After mutual salutations, he proceeded to address them very solemnly for some time, and having prayed for them, shook hands with each of them, who were bathed in tears, and parted from him as from a common parent. The following day, April 28th, according to his desire, all the ministers in the jurisdiction of Geneva came to him, whom he also addressed: "I avow," he said, "that I have lived united with you, brethren, in the strictest bonds of true and sincere affection, and I take my leave of you with the same feelings. If you have at any

* See in the Appendix. Speaking of his will, Bayle, the great Infidel philosopher, says:—" For a man who had acquired so great a reputation and authority, to content himself with a hundred crowns a-year salary, and after having lived till near fifty-five years of age with the greatest frugality, to leave behind him no more than three hundred crowns, his library included, is something so heroical, that it must be stupidity itself not to admire it. To conclude, such a will as this of Calvin's, and such a disinterestedness is a thing so very extraordinary, as might make even those who cast their eyes on the philosophers of ancient Greece, say of him, *non inveni tantam fidem in Israel.* I have not found so great faith, no, not in Israel." See his Dictionary, fol. 2. art. Calvin.

time found me harsh or peevish under my affliction, I entreat your forgiveness." Having shook hands with them, we took leave of him, says Beza, " with sad hearts and by no means with dry eyes."

"The remainder of his days," as Beza informs us, "Calvin passed in almost perpetual prayer. His voice was interrupted by the difficulty of his respiration; but his eyes (which to the last retained their brilliancy,) uplifted to heaven, and the expression of his countenance, shewed the fervour of his supplications. His doors," Beza proceeds to say, "must have stood open day and night, if all had been admitted who, from sentiments of duty and affection, wished to see him, but as he could not speak to them, he requested they would testify their regard by praying for him, rather than by troubling themselves about seeing him. Often, also, though he ever shewed himself glad to receive me, he intimated a scruple respecting the interruption thus given to my employments; so thrifty was he of time which ought to be spent in the service of the church."

On the 19th of May, being the day the ministers assembled, and when they were accustomed to take a meal together, Calvin requested that they should sup in the hall of his house. Being seated, he was with much difficulty carried into the hall: "I have come, my brethren," said he, "to sit with you, for the last time, at this table." But, before long, he said—" I must be carried to my bed;" adding, as he looked round upon them, with a serene and pleasant countenance, "these walls will not prevent my union with you in spirit, although my body be absent." He never afterwards left his bed. On the 27th of May, about eight o'clock in the evening, the symptoms of dissolution came suddenly on. In the full possession of his reason, he continued to speak, until, without a struggle or a gasp, his lungs ceased to play, and this great luminary of the Reformation set, with the setting sun, to rise again in the firmament of heaven. The dark shadows of mourning settled upon the city. It was with the whole people a night of lamentation and tears. All could bewail their loss; the city her best citizen, the church her renovator and guide, the college her founder, the cause of reform its ablest champion, and every family a friend and comforter. It was necessary to exclude the crowds of visitors who came to behold his remains, lest the occasion might be misrepresented. At two o'clock in the afternoon of Sabbath, his body, enclosed in a wooden coffin, and followed by the syndics, senators, pastors, professors, together with almost the whole city, weeping as they went, was carried to the common burying ground, without pomp. According to his request, no monument was erected to his memory; a plain stone, without any inscription, being all that covered the remains of Calvin.

Such was Calvin in his life and in his

death. The place of his burial is unknown, but where is his fame unheard?

As Cato said of the proposed statue for himself, so may it be said of Calvin's monument: "There are so many monuments in this world of ours, that it may be much better if people ask, Where is Cato's monument, than to say, There it is." So is it with Calvin. He hath built himself a monument in the hearts and lives of millions, more enduring and more glorious than any columns of stone or brass.

> What needs great Calvin, for his honoured bones,
> The labour of an age in piled stones?
> Or that his hallowed relics should be hid
> Under a star y-pointing pyramid?
> Dear son of Memory, great heir of Fame,
> What need'st thou such weak witness of thy name?
> Thou, in our reverence and astonishment,
> Hast built thyself a live-long monument.*

To conclude, we may unite with a late episcopal reviewer of the character of Calvin, in hoping that the time is not far distant, when new Horsleys will be raised up to

---

* The following are the lines of Beza, in reference to Calvin's tomb:

> Why, in this humble and unnoticed tomb,
> Is Calvin laid, the dread of falling Rome,
> Mourned by the good, and by the wicked feared,
> By all who knew his excellence revered;
> From whom ev'n Virtue's self might virtue learn,
> And young and old its value may discern?
> 'Twas modesty, his constant friend on earth,
> That laid this stone, unsculptured with a name.
> O happy turf, enriched with Calvin's worth,
> More lasting far than marble is thy fame.

break in pieces the arrows of calumny, and to make all the followers of the Prince of Peace and truth ashamed to join the ranks of the infidels, in using the poisoned weapons of shameless detraction for the purpose of vilifying the character of one of the most holy—the most undaunted—the most laborious, and the most disinterested followers of a crucified Redeemer."*

## SECTION IX.

#### A SUPPLEMENTARY VINDICATION OF THE ORDINATION OF CALVIN.

In preparing this vindication of the character and life of Calvin, I was not led to notice the question which has been raised by his enemies, the Romanists and Prelatists, whether Calvin was ever ordained. This question did not fall under the general view of Calvin's life and character, which it was my object to take. The question had been often met, and triumphantly answered; and appeared to me to possess little interest or importance at the present time. Circumstances, however, have changed. The baseless attempts to fasten upon Calvin an approval of diocesan episcopacy, having been completely foiled—and the calumnies against his general character having been repelled—his ene-

* The Rev. Mr. Sibson, A. B., of Trinity Coll. Dublin, in his Transl. of Beza's Life, p. 118, 119.

mies have taken refuge in this forlorn hope, and are now heard on every side exclaiming, "ah, but Calvin, after all, was never ordained." It is really amusing to see the baby-artifices which suffice these profound scholars! these inimitable logicians! these exclusive possessors of all grace! "Calvin was never ordained," say our prelatic friends. "Calvin was never ordained," shout the Romanists. "And Mr. Smyth has not even attempted to prove this all-important fact," they both proclaim in loudest chorus. We will now, then, meet these same confident boasters, and accept their challenge to discuss this question.

And, in the first place, we remark, that it is a matter of no practical importance whatever, to Presbyterians, whether Calvin was or was not ordained. This whole outcry is mere noise, *vox et præterea nihil,* got up in order to drown the voice of reason, and turn away attention from evident defeat.

Let it then be fully understood that the validity of Presbyterian ordination depends, IN NO MANNER OR DEGREE, upon the ordination of Calvin. He may have been ordained or not ordained, while of our ordination there can be no manner of doubt. Were the validity of our ordinations made to depend upon the personal succession of a line of single ordainers—were Calvin a link in that line—and were our present chain connected with him—then, indeed, there would be some sense and some force in the objections made against Calvin's ordination. It is on this ground we boldly deny that any valid *prelatical* ordination exists, or can be shown to exist, either in the Romish, Anglican, or American Episcopal churches. But we hold to no such doctrine. Our ordination depends not upon one prelate, but upon many presbyters. So that even if invalidity could be shown to attach to any one of the number of presbyters officiating in any given case, it does not affect the whole, and consequently does not injure that ordination which is given by the whole. Did Calvin ever ordain ALONE? Did Calvin ordain *alone* all those from whom our present ordinations spring? Preposterous assumption! which all the boldness of reckless malignity has never dared to make.

Suppose, then, that Calvin, while unordained, had united with the presbytery of Geneva, in conferring ordination upon others. Were not the others, Farel and Coraud, ordained, and ordained too by Romish prelates? Were not Luther and Zuinglius, and many others, prelatically ordained? And, subtracting, therefore, the invalid co-operation of Calvin from the ceremony, was there not still validity enough to secure a valid result? On the ground of scripture, of reason, and of the theory of presbyterian ordination, most assuredly there was. And whatever our opponents may choose to say of the validity of presbyterian ordination *generally*, they cannot, without betraying absolute absurdity, affirm that it depends, in any degree, upon the fact of Calvin's ordination. This whole question, therefore, is merely one of literary curiosity and historical research.

But we proceed a step further, and affirm that Calvin's character and authority as a minister of Jesus Christ, did not depend upon his ordination. Ordination does not confer upon any man either the character or the authority of a minister of Christ. The qualifications which fit any man for this high office can be imparted only by God, through Christ, and by the effectual operation of the Holy Spirit. Without these, no man is a fit subject for ordination, which presupposes their existence. The authority to preach the gospel arises also from that commission which Christ has given to all those whom he—as the only Head of the Church, to whom all power in heaven and on earth has been given—has qualified for the work. It is a blasphemous assumption, in any church or body of men, to claim the power of imparting to others, either the qualifications or the authority to preach the gospel. Ordination, therefore, is not in itself absolutely essential to a true ministry, since there may be the qualifications and the authority to use them, without it. Ordination is merely the appointed method whereby any given branch of the Church declares their belief that the individual ordained, is qualified and authorized by God to preach the gospel: and whereby they commend him to all those for whom they act, as worthy of their confidence, and entitled to all the respect and consideration due to a minister of Christ. Ordination, therefore, is essential to the *regularity*, but not to the *validity* of the ministry. And should any church have such unbounded confidence in the qualifications and call of any man for the office, as to allow him to minister among them without a special ordination, he would be no less certainly a minister, because admitted in an unusual way to the exercise of his gifts and calling. In ordinary circumstances, of course, no such case could occur. We speak hypothetically. But is it true that Calvin was never ordained? —then do our remarks apply, in all their strength, to him. Who ever doubted his qualifications for the ministry? Not, surely, the ministers and magistrates of Geneva, when they, almost by violence, compelled him to enter upon its duties. Having, then, as the whole reformed world believe, the qualifications and call which fitted him for the ministry, Calvin had also the authority of Christ for engaging in its work. And if the churches thought it unnecessary that he should be formally set apart by ordination, Calvin's authority as a minister of Christ is not the less, but even the more evident; since it was believed by all to be accredited by *extraordinary* gifts and calling.*

* See these views fully and literally sustained by the Confession of the French Churches, article xxxi., Quick's Synod, vol. 1. p. xiii.; and by many other reformed bodies and authors as given in Henderson's Rev. & Consid. p. 252-263.

But still further, we affirm, that Calvin was authorized to preach by the Romish Church itself. He received the tonsure at the hands of the Romish prelate, which is the first part of the ceremony of ordination, and qualifies for holding benefices and cures. The hair then cut from the crown of the head, shows, as is taught by Romanists, that the individual partakes of the sovereignty of Jesus Christ.* In virtue of this office and authority, "it is certain" that John Calvin delivered some sermons at Pont L'Eveque, before he left France.† He had ordination sufficient, therefore, in the judgment of the Romish Church, to warrant his preaching. And since the power this church professes to give in ordination for the priesthood, is idolatrous and blasphemous,‡ and is not attempted or believed in by the reformed churches, Calvin received from the Romish Church all that authority, which is deemed sufficient for those duties recognised by protestants as proper and peculiar to the ministry.

But we advance still further in our argument, and assert that it is a matter of the most certain inference that Calvin was ordained in the Reformed Church, and by the presbytery of Geneva.

That a presbytery existed at Geneva, before Calvin reached that city, is beyond

---

\* See Broughton's Eccl. Dict. Fol. 2. 468.
† Beza's Life.
‡ The offering of the sacrifice of the body and blood of Christ, by transubstantiation.

doubt. Beza expressly declares that, when Farel, by his denunciation, overcame the purpose of Calvin to pass by Geneva, "Calvin, affrighted by this terrible denunciation, gave himself up to the will of the presbytery and the magistrates." (Presbyterii et magistratus voluntati.)\*

That it was the established and uniform belief of the reformers, that ordination, in the ordinary circumstances of the church, was necessary and very important, and that their practice was consistent with this belief, is equally certain. Unless this is denied, it is unnecessary to produce the proofs which are at hand.†

Nay more, it is beyond doubt that this was the judgment not only of all the other reformers, but also of Calvin himself. He insists, in many parts of his Institutes, (his earliest theological work,) upon the importance and necessity of ordination by the imposition of hands. (See Book IV. chap. iii. § 16, and chap. iv. § 6, 10, 14.) These sentiments, which Calvin had published just before going to Geneva, he ever after held, as is manifest in all the subsequent editions of this work, and in the Confession of the French Churches, which he drew up, and in which ordina⸺ is declared to be essential to a regular ministry.

The inference, therefore, is unavoidable, that since there was a presbytery at Geneva

\* Calvin Op. folio. 1.
† See Seaman's Vind. of the judgment of the Reformed Church concerning Ordination. London, 1647.

when Calvin went there, since all the reformers, and Calvin in particular, insisted on the necessity and scripturality of ordination; and since Calvin is expressly said to have given himself up to the presbytery, he must have been, and he was, ordained. No particular record of the time and manner of his consecration is necessary. There is circumstantial evidence more than sufficient to establish the fact in any court of law.

But still further. Calvin himself bears witness that he was ordained. Thus in his preface to his Commentaries on the Psalms, he says:—"As David was raised from the sheepfold to the highest dignity of government, so God has dignified me, derived from an obscure and humble origin, with the high and honourable office of minister and preacher of the Gospel."* But, since Calvin himself publicly and constantly taught the necessity of ordination to the ministry, in making this declaration he asserts also the *fact* of his ordination. Thus, also, when Cardinal Sadolet attacked the character of his ministry, he formally defended it in a long epistle addressed to that distinguished man.† In this defence he says: "sed quum ministerium meum quod Dei vocatione fundatum ac sancitum fuisse non dubito, per latus meum sauciari videam, perfidia erit, non patientia, si taceam hic atque dissimulem. Doctoris pri-

* Hoc tamen honorifico numere dignatus est, ut evangelii præco essem ac minister. Op. Tom. iii.

† Ad J. Sadoletum Responio, &c., in Op. Tom. viii. p. 105, &c.

mum, deinde pastoris munere in ecclesia illa functus sum. Quod eam provinciam suscepi, legitimæ fuisse vocationis jure meo contendo." "Hoc ergo ministerium ubi a Domino esse constiterit," &c. That is, "when I see *my ministry*, which I doubt not was founded and sanctioned by the vocation of God, wounded through my side, it would be perfidy and not patience, if I should remain silent and dissemble in such a case. I filled (or enjoyed the honor of) the office, first of professor, and afterwards of pastor in that church, and I contend that I accepted of that charge, having the authority of a lawful vocation." "Since then, my ministry has been established by the Lord," &c. If, then, the testimony of Calvin—published to the world, in the face of the Reformed Churches, and in full view of their sentiments and practice on the subject of ordination, in both which he concurred—can be relied on, then is his introduction to the ministry by a regular ordination, beyond all controversy certain.

But still further. We have the evidence of the reformers and reformed churches themselves, that Calvin was ordained. No one stood higher among them as a minister and a leader. He was chosen moderator of the presbytery at Geneva, and continued to fill that office till his death. He sat in the synods of the Swiss churches. When driven from Geneva, he retired to Strasburgh, where he was again constrained to enter upon the duties of a professor and a pastor, by the agency of those distinguished men, Bucer, Capito, Hedio, Niger, and Sturmius. Bucer, also, in a letter addressed to him in 1536, expressly calls him "my brother and fellow minister." Now all these reformers, as we have seen, held that ordination was both scriptural and necessary; and since Calvin himself was of the same opinion, we must regard their testimony to his ministerial character and standing, as proof positive of their belief that he was regularly ordained.

Beza, in his life of Calvin, seems to declare that he was ordained as plainly as language could do it. He says:—"Calvinus sese presbyterii et magistratus voluntati permisit; quorum suffragiis, accedente plebis consensu, delectus non concionatur tantum (hoc autem primum recusarat) sed etiam sacrarum literarum doctor, quod unum admittebat, est designatus, A. D. MDXXXVI." That is, "Calvin surrendered himself to the disposal of the presbytery and magistrates, by whose votes, (the people having previously expressed their willingness,) having been chosen not only preacher, (which office he had, however, at first declined,) but also professor of divinity, he was set apart or inducted into office, in the year 1536." Now the very office and duty of a presbytery is, among other things, to admit and ordain men to the ministry. But Calvin was admitted to the ministry by a presbytery composed of reformers who strongly insisted upon the importance of the rite of ordination. Calvin, also, concurred in their views of this ordinance, as introductory to the ministry. And Beza says, that having been elected pastor by the people, and having been approved by the votes of the presbytery, " he was set apart," that is, in the regular way, by ordination. Beza never dreamt that, in after times, a fact so necessarily implied in his statement, and in all the circumstances of the case, could or would be, questioned.

This clear testimony of Beza is confirmed by that of Junius, the learned Professor of Divinity in Leyden. In opposition to Bellarmine, he affirms that the reformers who preceded Calvin, held and practised presbyterian ordination, and that by some of these, his predecessors, Calvin was himself ordained.*

Certain it is that neither Romanists nor prelatists, at that day, ever questioned the fact that Calvin was ordained in the manner of the Reformed Church. The Romanists did not. Cardinal Bellarmine says that " neither Luther, nor Zuingle, nor Calvin, were bishops, (*i. e.* prelates,) but only presbyters;† thus evidently assuming as undeniable that they were all presbyters, and therefore ordained as such. Cardinal Sadolet seems also, from the controversy between him and Calvin, fully to have admitted Calvin's ordination according to the order of the Reformed Church, but to have denied the validity of such orders, because administered out of the

* Animadversiones in Bellarm. Controv. V Lib. cap. 3, in Dr. Miller on Min. p. 407.
† Controv. V Lib. cap. 3, in Dr. Miller on Min.

Romish Church. And hence the object of Calvin, in his reply, is not to establish the *fact* of his ordination, but the validity and scripturality of the orders of the Reformed Church.

Neither did prelatists then question the ministerial character and standing, and the consequent ordination, of Calvin. Dr. John Philpot, archdeacon of Winchester, martyr in 1555, in proving that the Reformed is the true church, by the 'spirit of wisdom, that the adversaries thereof could never be able to resist,' says, 'Where is there one of you all that ever hath been able to answer any of the godly, learned *ministers* of Germany, who have disclosed your counterfeit religion. Which of you all, at this day, is able to answer Calvin's Institutes, who is *minister* of Geneva?' To this his popish inquisitor, Dr. Saverson, replied, not by denying the ordination or ministerial character of Calvin, but by blackening the character of the reformers generally—'a godly minister, indeed, of receipt of cutpurses and runagate traitors,' &c. 'I am sure,' replied Philpot, 'you blaspheme that godly man, and that godly church *where he is a minister*, as it is your church's con dition, when you cannot answer men by learning, to oppress them with blasphemies and false reports.'\* This title he proceeds to give Calvin again in the very next sentence.† Bishop Jewell, the authorized ex-

\* See Examinations and Writings of Philpot, Parker Society edition, p. 45, 46.
† Foxe's Exam. of Philpot.

pounder of the sentiments of the English Church, replies to the Jesuit Harding, "touching Mr. Calvin, it is a great wrong untruly to represent so reverend a father and so worthy an ornament of the church of God. If you had ever known the order of the church of Geneva, and had seen four thousand people or more, receiving the holy mysteries together at one communion, you could not, without your great shame and want of modesty, thus untruly have published to the world, that by Mr. Calvin's doctrine the sacraments are superfluous."—Defence of the Apology; see in Richmond's Fathers of the English Church, vol. viii. p. 680. Such also were the views entertained by Archbishop Cranmer, Bishop Hooper, Bishop Hall, and many others. Hooker implies the ordination and perfect ministerial standing of Calvin, in all that he says of him. He calls him "incomparably the wisest man (*i. e.* minister) the French Church did enjoy, since the hour it had him." Speaking of the Genevan clergy, he calls them, " pastors of their souls," and then adds, " Calvin being admitted *one* of their preachers," that is, one of these pastors, for they had no preachers, except their regularly ordained ministers, " wherefore taking to him two of *the other* ministers," &c.*

Bullinger also, the cotemporary of Calvin, of whom it is said that " all the fathers of the English reformation held him in great esteem," and that " he did much service in

* Eccl. Pol. Pref. vol. i. p. 158, 159, Keble's ed.

the English Church;" to whom Bishops Grindal and Horn, in a joint letter to him, "attribute chiefly the favourable change which had taken place in the feelings of the people toward the church;"* and whose catechism was selected by the University of Oxford, as one of those books which the tutors were required to use; most explicitly sustains the ministerial character of Calvin. In a work published by order of the convocation of the English Church in 1586, *cum gratia et privilegio regiæ majestatis,* and as a manual for preachers,† he speaks of Calvin in these terms: "John Calvin, a godly and learned man, who with great commendation teacheth in the church at this day, my fellow minister, and most well-beloved and dear brother."‡

"Stancarus also, the Polish reformer, wrote a work 'Adversus Henricum Bullingerum, Petrum Martyrem et Joannem Calvinum, et reliquos Tigurinæ ac Genevensis ecclesiæ *ministros,* ecclesiæ Dei perturbatores,' etc., Basle, 1547. This work was replied to by Semler, and is referred to by Bishop Jewell in a letter to this Swiss reformer. Now here we have Calvin expressly denominated *a minister* by a Romanist, in a controversial work written against him, and in the same sense in which Bullinger and Peter Martyr are called ministers. And it

* Strype's Mem. II. 1. p. 531, 532, Oxf. ed. Strype's Grindal, p. 156, Oxf. ed.
† Wilkin's Concilia, &c., vol. iv. p. 321, 322.
‡ Bullinger on the Sacraments, Cambridge, 1840, p. 287.

remains to be shown, that Roman Catholic theologians are in the habit of applying the term 'minister' to persons whom they believe to be in no sense or manner ordained."* In " A Christian Letter of certain English Protestants, unfeigned favourers of the present state of religion authorized and professed in England, unto that reverend and learned man, Mr. R. Hooker," written in 1590, it is said, " the reverend fathers of our church call Mr. Calvin one of the best writers (Whitgift Def. of Ans. p. 390); *a reverend father* and a worthy ornament of the church of God, (Jewel Apol. Def. of, pt. II. p. 149; read any English writer defending the Church of England, and namely Fulke against Stapleton fortress, p. 71; read Apol. Angl.) not only defending the same doctrine, but also discharging him of slanderous reports wrongfully laid against him; knowing that by defaming the persons of ministers, the devil of old time laboured to overthrow the gospel of Christ." See quoted at length in Hanbury's edition of Hooker's Works, vol. i. p. 22, 23. The whole is very strong. See also Wordsworth's Eccl. Biogr. vol. iv. p. 269, vol. v. p. 544, &c. Of the opinion of the English Church, as to the ordination of John Calvin in 1586, there can, therefore, be no longer any question.

Such, then, is the accumulated evidence in proof of the certain and necessary ordination of Calvin. It can only be denied by those

* See Zurich Letters, 1558—1579, Parker Society, p. 127.

who are willing, for sectarian purposes, to shut their eyes against the clearest light. It is asserted by Calvin himself, by Beza, and by Junius. It is implied as necessary in the practice of the whole Reformed Church, of which Calvin approved, and which the presbytery of Geneva must have carried out. It was allowed by Romanists and prelatists of his own age, and is implied in the estimation in which he was regarded by the whole Reformed Church.

But even were the ordination of Calvin doubtful, we have shown that he was so far ordained by the Romish Church as to be authorized to preach; that his authority as a minister depends not on the ceremony of ordination; and that, inasmuch as our present orders are in no degree dependent upon his, their validity is in no way connected with the fact or certainty of Calvin's ordination.

While the validity of Romish and Prelatical ordination hangs upon the baseless assumption of an unbroken line of personal successors of the Apostles—a mere figment of the imagination, and without any foundation in Scripture, reason, or fact—our ordination is traced up directly to Christ and his Apostles; is based upon the clear evidence of Scripture, and the undoubted practice of the primitive Christians; and is transmitted, not through one line, but through many, and not through any one order of prelates, but through the whole body of pastors and ministers who have successively existed in every age of the Church.

# APPENDIX I.

### THE WILL OF JOHN CALVIN.

In the name of the Lord.—Amen. In the year 1564, and 25th day of April, I, Peter Chenalat, citizen and notary of Geneva, do witness and declare, that I was sent for by that excellent character, John Calvin, minister of the word of God in this church of Geneva, and enrolled citizen of the same, who, being indisposed in body, but sound in mind, said he was desirous to make his testament, and to express the judgment of his last will; and requested me to take it down, and write what he should dictate and declare by word of mouth; which I profess I immediately did, and wrote down word by word as he pronounced and dictated, without omission or addition, in the following form, dictated by him:

In the name of the Lord.—Amen. I, John Calvin, minister of the word of God in the church of Geneva, finding myself so much oppressed and afflicted with various diseases, that I think the Lord God has determined speedily to remove me out of this world, have ordered to be made and written, my testament, and declaration of my last will, in form and manner following: First, I give thanks to God, that taking compassion on me whom he had created and placed in this world, he not only delivered me by his power out of the deep darkness of idolatry, into which I was plunged, that he might bring me into the light of his gospel, and make me a partaker of the doctrine of salvation, of which I was most unworthy; that with the same goodness and mercy he has graciously and kindly borne with my multiplied transgressions and sins, for which I deserved to be rejected and cut off by him; and has also exercised towards me such great compassion and clemency, that he has condescended to use my labour in preaching and publishing the truth of his gospel. I also testify and declare, that it is my full intention to pass the remainder of my life in the same faith and religion, which he has delivered to me by his gospel; having no other defence or refuge of salvation than his gratuitous adoption, on which alone my safety depends. I also embrace with my whole heart the mercy which he exercises towards me for the sake of Jesus Christ, atoning for my crimes by the merits of his death and passion, that in this way satisfaction may be made for all my transgressions and offences, and the remembrance of them blotted out. I further testify and declare that, as a suppliant, I humbly implore of him to grant me to be so washed and purified by the blood of that sovereign

Redeemer, shed for the sins of the human race, that I may be permitted to stand before his tribunal in the image of the Redeemer himself. I likewise declare, that according to the measure of grace and mercy which God has vouchsafed me, I have diligently made it my endeavour, both in my sermons, writings, and commentaries, purely and uncorruptly to preach his word, and faithfully to interpret his sacred Scriptures. I testify and declare, that in all the controversies and disputes, which I have conducted with the enemies of the gospel, I have made use of no craftiness, nor corrupt and sophistical arts, but have been engaged in defending the truth with candour and sincerity.

But, alas! my study, and my zeal, if they deserve the name, have been so remiss and languid, that I confess innumerable things have been wanting in me to discharge the duties of my office in an excellent manner; and unless the infinite bounty of God had been present, all my study would have been vain and transient. I also acknowledge that unless the same goodness had accompanied me, the endowments of mind bestowed upon me by God, must have made me more and more chargeable with guilt and inactivity before his tribunal. And on these grounds I witness and declare, that I hope for no other refuge of salvation than this alone—that since God is a Father of mercy, he will show himself a Father to me, who confess myself a miserable sinner. Further, I will, after my departure out of this life, that my body be committed to the earth in that manner, and with those funeral rites, which are usual in this city and church, until the day of the blessed resurrection shall come. As for the small patrimony which God has bestowed upon me, and which I have determined to dispose of in this will, I appoint Anthony Calvin, my very dearly beloved brother, my heir, but only as a mark of respect. Let him take charge of, and keep as his own, my silver goblet, which was given me as a present by Mr. Varanne: and I desire he will be content with it. As for the residue of my property, I commit it to his care with this request, that he restore it to his children at his death. I bequeath also to the school for boys, ten golden crowns, to be given by my brother and legal heir, and to poor strangers the same sum. Also to Jane, daughter of Charles Costans, and of my half-sister by the paternal side, the sum of ten crowns. Furthermore, I wish my heir to give, on his death, to Samuel and John, sons of my said brother, my nephews, out of my estate, each forty crowns, after his death; and to my nieces Ann, Susan, and Dorothy, each thirty golden crowns. To my nephew David, as a proof of his light and trifling conduct, I bequeath only twenty-five golden crowns.

This is the sum of all the patrimony and property which God hath given me, as far as I am able to ascertain, in books, movables, my whole household furniture, and all

APPENDIX. 85

other goods and chattels. Should it however prove more, I desire it may be equally distributed between my nephews and nieces aforesaid, not excluding my nephew David, should he, by the favour of God, return to a useful manner of life.

Should it, however, exceed the sum already written, I do not think it will be attended with much difficulty, especially after paying my just debts, which I have given in charge to my said brother, in whose fidelity and kindness I confide. On this account I appoint him executor of this my last testament with Laurence de Normandie, a character of tried worth, giving them full power and authority, without a more exact command and order of court, to make an inventory of my goods. I give them also power to sell my movables, that from the money thus procured they may fulfil the conditions of my above-written will, which I have set forth and declared this 25th of April, in the year of our Lord 1564.

JOHN CALVIN.

When I, Peter Chenalat, the above-mentioned notary, had written this last will, the same John Calvin immediately confirmed it by his usual subscription and hand-writing. On the following day, April 26th, 1564, the same tried character, John Calvin, commanded me to be called, together with Theodore Beza, Raymond Chauvet, Michael Cops, Louis Enoch, Nicholas Colladon, James de Bordes, ministers and preachers of the word of God in this church of Geneva, and also the excellent Henry Scringer, professor of arts, all citizens of Geneva, and in their presence he hath declared and testified that he dictated to me this his will, in the words and form above written. He ordered me also to recite it in their hearing, who had been called for that purpose, which I profess to have done, with a loud voice, and in an articulate manner. After thus reading it aloud, he testified and declared it to be his last will and testament, and desired it to be ratified and confirmed. As a testimony and corroboration of this, he requested them all to witness the same will with their hands. This was immediately done by them on the day and year above written, at Geneva, in the street called the Canons, in the house of the said testator. In proof and witness of this I have written and subscribed with my own hand, and sealed, with the common seal of our supreme magistrate, the will above mentioned.

P. Chenalat.

# APPENDIX II.

### CALVIN'S VIEWS OF PRELACY.

On this subject we will present to our readers, the letters of the Rev. Dr. Miller in reply to Bishop Ives, which appeared in the Presbyterian in January, 1842.

#### LETTER I.

To the Editor of the Presbyterian.

REVEREND AND DEAR BROTHER—The following letter, and another which you will receive in a few days, were written a number of weeks ago, and sent to Lincolnton, in North Carolina, for insertion in the "Lincoln Republican," a weekly journal printed in that town. Very unexpectedly to me, the editor of that paper, after publishing Bishop Ives's letter, refused to give admission to my reply. On learning this, I requested the friend to whose care my communications had been sent, to transmit them to the "Watchman of the South," in whose pages they would be likely to be seen by a large number of those who had been readers of the "Lincoln Republican." But as Bishop Ives's letter has been republished in at least one paper in your city, and as in my reply to an attack in that paper, which you were so good as to publish, I referred to the letters which had been sent to North Carolina for further light on the same subject, I hope you will do me the favour to give insertion in the Presbyterian to the first letter, which you will receive herewith; and also to the second, which, with the permission of Providence, will reach you next week.

I make no apology, Mr. Editor, for the trouble which I have given you, for several weeks past, in consequence of these ecclesiastical polemics. I regret them as much as any one can do. They were not of my seeking. I am not conscious on this, or on any other occasion, of having ever gone into the field of denominational controversy, excepting when forced into it by fidelity to my beloved Church, and to her Head, my Master in heaven. To that high responsibility, however irksome controversy may be, especially at my time of life, I hope I shall never be suffered to be recreant. It would be much more agreeable to me to have no warfare but with the open enemies of our "common salvation;" but surely complaints of "attack" come with rather an ill grace from those who scarcely ever issue a paper without loading it with offensive missiles against all who are out of their pale. It has often amused me to see what a morbid sensibility to what they called "attacks," was manifested by those who were constantly dealing around them "firebrands and arrows," and professing at

# APPENDIX. 89

the same time, in words, to be "fierce for moderation," and "furious for peace." I am, my dear sir, very respectfully yours,
SAMUEL MILLER.
PRINCETON, *January* 24, 1842.

---

To the Editor of the Lincoln Republican.

SIR—It was not until this day that I saw, in your paper of the 10th instant, a letter from Bishop Ives, in reply to a letter from me, directed to a clerical friend in your neighbourhood, and published in your paper a few weeks before.

My letter was a *private one*, and published altogether without my consent. I kept no copy of it, and while I distinctly remember its general substance, I have not the least recollection of its language. The Bishop complains of the language, as strongly characterized by *asperity* and *positiveness*. As I have never seen even the printed copy, as it appeared in your paper, I am wholly unable to make any other reply to this charge, than to say, that, as I felt *strongly* on the subject, and was perfectly *confident* that the allegations which I opposed were altogether unfounded, I think it probable, that in a *private letter* to a friend, I expressed myself in terms which would have been modified if I had felt myself to be writing for the public eye. I had an interview with Bishop Ives, in this place, since the date of his letter; but as I had not the least knowledge, at that time of the publication of my own letter, or of his reply to it, nothing, of course, respecting the matter passed at that interview.

More than two months ago, a correspondent in North Carolina informed me that Bishop Ives, in a public discourse delivered a short time before, alleged that the celebrated reformer, Calvin, had avowed a belief in the divine institution of Episcopacy, and had requested to receive Episcopal ordination from the bishops of England. My correspondent requested me to inform him whether there was any foundation for this statement. I ventured, without hesitation, to assure him that there was not, and that no well-informed person could possibly make it. I have no recollection of having impeached the honesty or the veracity of the reverend preacher; for I had no doubt that he made the statement on evidence which he deemed sufficient; and I have still no doubt that he verily believed what he stated to be strictly true. But I meant to express, and presume I *did* express, strong confidence that the representation which he made was entirely incorrect. Bishop Ives is equally confident that his representation was well founded; and, in his reply to my published letter, has made statements which he seems to think perfectly decisive, and which, I dare say, many others will deem equally decisive, in support of his representation. And yet I will again assert, and hope I shall make it appear to the satisfaction of every candid reader, that that representation is destitute of all solid support in historical verity.

The first testimony which Bishop Ives adduces in support of his former statement, is in the following words: " In his commentary upon 1 Tim. iv. 14, a passage so much relied upon by Presbyterians, he gives an interpretation which makes it perfectly consistent with the *Episcopal* character of Timothy."

The passage, in our common translation, reads thus: " Neglect not the gift that is in thee, which was given thee by prophecy, with the laying on of the hands of the presbytery."

Calvin's commentary is as follows: " He admonishes him that he should employ the grace with which he was endowed for the edification of the Church. For it is not the will of the Lord that those talents should perish, or be uselessly buried in the earth, which he has deposited with any one to be profitably used. To *neglect* a gift, is, through sloth and negligence, to leave it unemployed; so that, given up, as it were, to rust, it is worn out in no useful service. Therefore let each of us consider what abilities he has, that he may sedulously apply them to some use. He says that the grace was *given to him by prophecy*. How? Doubtless (as we said before) because the Holy Spirit, by revelation, had appointed Timothy to be set apart to the office of a pastor; for he had not been chosen only by man's judgment, as is customary, but by the previous declaration of the

Spirit. He says that it was conferred with *the laying on of hands;* by which is meant that, in addition to the ministerial office, he was furnished also with the necessary gifts. It was a settled custom with the Apostles to ordain ministers with the imposition of hands; and, indeed, concerning this rite, its origin and meaning, I have treated at some length before, and a full account may be found in the Institutes. *Presbytery*—Those who think that this is a collective name put for *the college of Presbyters,* in my opinion judge correctly. Although, all things considered, I confess there is another sense not unsuitable, viz. that it is the name of an *office.* The ceremony he has put for the act of ordination itself. Therefore the sense is, that Timothy, when called to the ministry by the voice of the prophets, and afterwards ordained by the customary rite, was, at the same time, furnished for the performance of his duties by the grace of the Holy Spirit—whence we infer that it was not an empty rite, for to that consecration which men represented figuratively by the imposition of hands, God imparted reality, (or ratification) by his Spirit."

This is Calvin's commentary on the passage in question, and it is the *whole* of it. He who can find any thing favourable to the *Episcopal* character of Timothy here, will be at no loss to find it in any document on earth. The only thing noticeable in its bearing on that point is the suggestion, that while

APPENDIX. 93

in the opinion of Calvin the term *Presbytery* means the bench or body of *Presbyters*, it *may* mean the name of an *office*. But surely this makes nothing in favour of the prelatical character of Timothy; for if this sense be admitted, then the statement will be that Timothy was ordained to the office of the *Presbyterate*, or was made a *Presbyter*.

The Bishop next produces a *fragment* from Calvin's commentary on Titus i. 5, which he thus translates: "We learn also from this place that there was not then such an *equality* among the ministers of the Church, but that some one *had the pre-eminence* in authority and counsel."

The candid reader will doubtless feel astonished when he reads this passage in connection with the context in which it stands—It is as follows:

"*Presbyters* or *Elders*, it is well known, are not so denominated on account of their *age*, since *young* men are sometimes chosen to this office, as, for instance, *Timothy;* but it has always been customary, in all ages, to apply this title, as a term of honour, to all rulers—and as we gather, from the first Epistle to Timothy, that there were *two kinds* of Elders, so here the context shows that no other than *teaching Elders* are to be understood; that is those who were ordained to *teach*, because the same persons are immediately afterwards called *Bishops*. It may be objected that too much power seems to be given to *Titus*, when the Apostle commands him to appoint ministers over all the churches. This, it may be said, is little less than kingly power; for, on this plan, the right of choice is taken away from the particular churches, and the right of judging in the case from the college of pastors—and this would be to profane the whole of the sacred discipline of the Church. But the answer is easy. Every thing was *not entrusted* to *Titus* as an individual, nor was he allowed to impose such Bishops on the churches as he pleased; but he was commanded to *preside* in the elections as a *Moderator*, as it is necessary for some one to do. This is a mode of speaking exceedingly common. Thus a Consul or Regent or Dictator is said to create Consuls, because he convenes assemblies for the purpose of making choice of them. So also Luke uses the same mode of speaking concerning Paul and Barnabas in the Acts of the Apostles; not that they alone authoritatively appointed pastors over the churches without their being tried or approved; but they ordained suitable men, who had been elected or chosen by the people. We learn also from this place, that there was not, then, *such* an equality among the ministers of the Church as was inconsistent with some one of them presiding in authority and counsel. This, however, is nothing like the tyrannical and profane *Prelacy* which reigns in the Papacy: the plan of the Apostles was altogether different."

Is the reader prepared to find Bishop Ives separating the last sentence but one in this paragraph from what preceded and what follows, and calling it a declaration in favour of *Episcopacy*, when its whole tenor is directly the other way? If the Bishop had read one page further on, he would have found in Calvin's commentary on verse 7th of the same chapter, the following still more explicit declarations:

" Moreover, this place abundantly teaches us that there is no difference between *Presbyters* and *Bishops*, because the Apostle now calls promiscuously by the second of these names those whom he had before called *Presbyters*—and indeed the argument which follows employs both names indifferently in the same sense, which *Jerome* hath observed, as well in his commentary on this passage, as in his Epistle to *Evagrius*. And hence we may see how more has been yielded to the opinions of men than was decent, because the style of the Holy Spirit being abrogated, a custom introduced by the will of man prevailed. I do not, indeed, disapprove of the opinion that, soon after the commencement of the Church, every college of Bishops had some one to act as *Moderator*. But that a name of office which God had given *in common to all*, should be transferred to *an individual alone*, the rest being *robbed of it*, was both *injurious* and *absurd*. Wherefore, so to pervert the language of the Holy Spirit as that the same expressions should convey a meaning to us different from that which he intended, partakes too much of *profane audacity*."

It is worthy of remark that the work which contains this passage was published in 1549, in the reign of *Edward* VI.; and when Calvin was carrying on a friendly correspondence with Archbishop *Cranmer*—yet he did not hesitate then to avow his Presbyterian sentiments.

Again; in his commentary on 1 Peter v. 1, written in 1551, and dedicated to *Edward* VI. of England, Calvin thus speaks:

"*Presbyters.*—by this title he designates pastors, and whoever were appointed to the government of the Church. And since Peter calls himself a *Presbyter*, like the rest, it is hence apparent that this name was common, which, indeed, from many other passages, appears still more clearly. Moreover, by this title he claimed to himself authority, as if he had said that he admonished pastors in his own right, because he was one of their number, for among *colleagues* there ought to be this mutual privilege: whereas if he had enjoyed any pre-eminence of authority among them, he might have urged that, and it would have been more pertinent to the occasion. But although he was an Apostle, yet he knew this gave him no authority over his colleagues, but that he was rather joined with the rest in a social office."

Bishop Ives, as a further proof that Calvin was persuaded of the Divine right of Prelacy, tells us that in his commentary on Galatians ii. 9, he represents it as " highly probable that St. James was *prefect* of the Church of Jerusalem." "Now," says he, "a *prefect* is a chief and permanent ruler of others." Here again the slightest inspection of what Calvin does really and truly say, will sufficiently refute this construction of his language. It is this:

"When the question is here concerning dignity, it may seem wonderful that *James* should be preferred to *Peter*. Perhaps that might have been done because he was the *president*, (præfectus) of the Church of Jerusalem. In regard to what may be included in the title of "Pillars," we know that it is so ordered in the nature of things, that those who excel others in talents, in prudence, or in other gifts, are also superior in authority. So in the Church of God, by how much any one excels in grace by so much ought he to be preferred in honour. For it is ingratitude, nay it is impiety, not to do homage to the Spirit of God wherever he appears in his gifts. Hence it is, that as a people cannot do without a pastor, so every assembly of pastors needs some one to act as *moderator* But it ought ever to be so ordered that he who is first of all should be a servant, according to Matthew xxiii. 12."

In his commentary on Acts xx. 28, written in 1560, a few years before his death, Calvin expresses himself thus: "Concerning the word *Bishop* it is observable that Paul gives this title to all the *Elders* of Ephesus; from which we may infer, that, according to Scripture, *Presbyters* differed, in no respect, from *Bishops;* but that it arose from *corruption,* and a *departure from primitive purity,* that those who held the first seats in particular cities began to be called *Bishops.* I say that it arose from *corruption,* not that it is an evil for some one in each college of pastors, to be distinguished above the rest; but because it is *intolerable presumption,* that men, in perverting the titles of Scripture to their own humour, do not hesitate to alter the meaning of the Holy Spirit."

The Bishop's extract from Calvin's work *De necessitate Reformandæ Ecclesiæ,* will also prove, when examined, quite as little to his purpose as any of the preceding. The passage, as given by him, is in the following words: "If they will give us such an hierarchy in which the bishops have such a preeminence as that they do not refuse to be subject to Christ, then I will confess that they are worthy of all anathemas, if any such shall be found who will not reverence it, and submit themselves to it with the utmost obedience."

The passage, as really found in Calvin's work is as follows:—After speaking of the hierarchy of the Romish Church; of its claims of *uninterrupted succession* from the apostles, which he turns into ridicule; and of the gross departure of the bishops from the spirit and rules of the gospel, he says: "If the Papists would exhibit to us such an hierarchy, as that the bishops should be so distinguished as not to refuse to be subject to

Christ; to rely on him as their only Head; to cherish fraternal union among themselves; and to be bound together by no other tie than his truth, then I should confess that there is no anathema of which *they* are not worthy, who should not regard such an hierarchy with reverence and obedience. But what likeness to such an one is borne by that spurious hierarchy, in which they (the Romanists) boast?" He then goes on inveighing against the arrogance and tyranny of the Bishop of Rome, by name, and showing how entirely different that system is from that to which Christ and his apostles gave their sanction, and even that which prevailed in the time of Cyprian.

It is well known that Calvin, in all his writings maintained that there were *Bishops* in the primitive Church; that every pastor of a congregation was a scriptural bishop; of course, he might well say, that if there were any who would not obey *such bishops* as were conformed to the will of Christ, they were worthy of all condemnation. Some have alleged indeed, that his use of the word *hierarchy,* (*hierarchiam*) in this passage, proves that he could have had reference to no other than a *prelatical* government; that the term is never applied to any other. This is an entire mistake. The word *hierarchy* simply implies *sacred* or *ecclesiastical government.* It may be applied with as much propriety to *Presbyterianism* or *Independency,* as to *Prelacy.* Calvin himself in his

*Institutions,* Book iv. chapter 5, speaks of that *hierarchy,* or *spiritual government,* which was left in the Church by the apostles, and which he expressly declares, in the same chapter, to be Presbyterian in its form.

Further, we are told, it seems, by *Durell,* in his "View of the Foreign Reformed Churches," that Calvin, in writing to an "old friend," speaks of the office of Bishop as of "divine institution or appointment." It is true that language of this kind is found in that letter, but the most cursory perusal of the whole letter, will banish from any candid mind the idea that Calvin is here speaking of diocesan or prelatical Episcopacy. Does not every intelligent reader know that that great Reformer believed and uniformly taught that the office of Bishop (that is, of the *primitive, parochial* bishop,) was a divine institution? It is evidently of this *parochial Episcopacy* that he speaks, when writing to his "old friend" in the language above quoted. The duties which he urges upon him, and the passages of Scripture which he quotes to enforce his counsel; all show that it is *that* Episcopacy alone which he maintains to be of divine appointment. A Prelatist might as well quote the fourth chapter of the Presbyterian Form of Government, in which it speaks of *Bishops,* as proof positive that it maintains the divine right of Prelacy, as adduce the language cited by Bishop Ives to prove that Calvin was an advocate for the divine institution of Prelatical Episcopacy.

APPENDIX. 101

Such is the clear, indubitable testimony that the illustrious Reformer of Geneva was guiltless of the charge which has been brought against him. It is manifest that, with perfect uniformity during the greater part of his public life, from 1535 to 1560, he steadfastly maintained the doctrine that the apostolic form of church government was Presbyterian, and not Prelatical: that even in works which he dedicated to the king of England and to the Lord Protector, the highest nobleman in the realm, he still firmly contended for the scriptural doctrine of ministerial parity. The more closely I examine his writings, the more confirmed is my persuasion, that nothing which wears a contrary aspect can be fairly produced from them.

II. The *second* allegation of Bishop Ives, is, that this eminent man *wished to introduce Prelacy into the Church of Geneva; and that he united with others in requesting the English Bishops to impart it to them.*

If I do not greatly mistake, this allegation also is capable of being completely refuted. But as I have already trespassed so far on the columns of your paper, I shall postpone to another week, the remarks and the testimony which I have to adduce in regard to that point. In the mean time, I am, Sir, with great respect, your obedient servant,

SAMUEL MILLER.

PRINCETON, *Nov.* 20*th*, 1841.

## LETTER II.

The second allegation of Bishop Ives is, that *Calvin was desirous of introducing diocesan Episcopacy into the Church of Geneva; and that he, with others, requested the bishops of England to impart it to them.*

I have expressed a strong confidence that this statement is utterly unfounded; and that it admits of satisfactory refutation. To attempt this refutation I now proceed.

And, in proceeding to the execution of this task, my first remark is, that, anterior to all search after testimony, the allegation is, *in itself, utterly incredible.* The character which the friends of Prelacy are fond of imputing to John Calvin, is that of an austere, fierce, tyrannical man, fond of power, and impatient of all opposition. His character, indeed, in this respect, has been much misunderstood, and shamefully misrepresented. A degree of magisterial intolerance has been ascribed to him, which he never manifested. Still it is true that he possessed *great decision of character,* and that in following his convictions, and labouring to attain his favourite objects, he was hardly ever exceeded by any man. In this, it is believed, all are agreed. Now if this man, who had such controlling influence in Geneva, had been desirous of introducing Prelacy into his own pastoral charge, and the neighbouring churches, who

# APPENDIX. 103

was there to prevent it? Surely not the *civil government*. The secular rulers had been accustomed to Prelacy all their lives, and would, no doubt, have regarded it with more favour than any other form of ecclesiastical regimen that could be proposed to them. Not his *ministerial colleagues*, for though they were by no means timid or pliant men, yet his influence over them seems to have been of the highest kind; and if Prelacy had been introduced, who can doubt that Calvin himself would have been the Prelate? Who else would have been thought of? To him all eyes would have been instantly directed. No one acquainted with the history of Luther, Calvin, and several of the leading Reformers, who acted with them, can hesitate a moment to believe, that a Bishop's chair was within the reach of every one of them, if he had only signified his wish to the effect, or even intimated his belief that such an office was warranted by the word of God.

But suppose in the face of all this improbability, that Calvin *did* wish to introduce Prelacy; what occasion had he to go to *England* for the purpose of obtaining it? Were there not several men who had been Bishops under the Papacy, who espoused the cause of the Reformation, and who would have been ready to lend their aid toward the consummation of the desired object? Besides, our Episcopal brethren tell us that the *Waldenses* always had bishops, in *their* sense of that title, among them. If so, where was the difficulty of Calvin and his colleagues obtaining the *Episcopal succession,* as the modern phrase is, from that body of pious believers? We know, indeed, that this assertion concerning the Waldenses is unfounded. They had no such bishops. They themselves, in their correspondence with *Oecolampadius,* in 1530, explicitly inform him that they had not; still, as an *argumentum ad hominem,* the argument is conclusive. Either there were no such bishops among that pious, devoted people, as Prelatists claim; or Calvin, who knew the Waldenses intimately, and had intercourse with them, acted a strange part in seeking an ecclesiastical favour from the British Church, which he might, quite as conveniently, to say the least, have obtained from churches in his native country, where many of them were settled, as well as in the Valleys of *Piedmont.*

But there is another fact bearing on the point, no less conclusive. The allegation is, that Calvin and his friends begged for Episcopal consecration from Archbishop *Cranmer,* in the reign of *Edward* VI., when that prelate was at the head of the ecclesiastical affairs of England. Now, in that very reign, when this wish and request must have been pending, as shown in a former letter, we find Calvin repeatedly publishing to the world his opposition to Prelacy, and his solemn conviction that the Scriptures laid down a different form of church order; and one of these publications, containing one of his strongest assertions in favour of Presbyterianism, he dedicated to the king of England, and sent to him by the hand of a special messenger; on the return of which messenger, Cranmer wrote to Calvin an affectionate letter, thanking him for his present, and expressing an opinion that he could not do better than often to write to the king. (*See Strype's Memorials of Cranmer, p.* 413.) How is it possible for these things to hang together? If Calvin was capable of writing and printing these things, and sending them by special messengers to the king, and to Archbishop Cranmer, at the very time when he was negotiating with Cranmer, to obtain from him an investiture of a different and opposite kind;—if he was capable of acting thus, it would be difficult to say, whether he was more of a knave or a fool. But I know not that any one, who was acquainted with the history or the writings of that eminent man, ever charged him with being either.

The first evidence that Bishop Ives adduces to support his allegation, that Calvin desired to obtain Prelatical Episcopacy for his own Church in Geneva, is drawn from his language in the Confession of Faith, which he composed in the name of the French Churches. The friends of Prelacy are heartily welcome to all the testimony which can be drawn from that confession. Every thing in it which bears upon this point is in the following words: "As to the true Church, we believe it ought to be governed according to the policy which our Lord Jesus Christ has established; that is, that there be Pastors, Elders and Deacons; that the pure doctrine may have its course; that vices may be corrected and repressed; that the poor and all other afflicted persons be succoured in their necessities; and that all the assemblies be made in the name of God, in which both great and small may be edified. We believe that all true pastors, in whatsoever place they be, have *the same authority* and an *equal power*, under one only Chief, only Sovereign, and universal Bishop Jesus Christ; and for that reason that no church ought to pretend to Sovereignty or Lordship over another." If this be evidence that Calvin wished to introduce Prelacy into those churches on the Continent, over which he had influence, then I know not what testimony means. The Confession is decisively anti-prelatical in its character throughout, and the churches which were organized on its basis, were as thoroughly Presbyterian as the Church of Scotland ever was. In the "Articles of ecclesiastical discipline," drawn up at the same time, it is declared that "a President in each Colloquy (or classis) or Synod shall be chosen with a common consent to preside in the Colloquy or Synod, and to do every thing that belongs to it; and the said office shall *end* with each Colloquy or Synod and Council." (*See Laval's History of the Reformation in France, Vol. I. p.* 118.)

Another source of proof on which Bishop Ives relies to show that Calvin wished for and endeavoured to obtain Prelacy from the English Church, is found in the language which he addressed to the clergy of Cologne, blaming them for attempting to depose their Archbishop, because he was friendly to the Reformation. But could not Calvin reprobate this conduct without believing in the divine institution of the office which the Archbishop held? Suppose Bishop Ives should become a Calvinist, as to his theological creed, and suppose the Episcopal Clergy of North Carolina should conspire on that account alone, to expel him from his diocese, might not the firmest Presbyterian in the State remonstrate against their conspiracy without being an advocate for the divine right of prelacy? Might he not consider it much better to retain, in an influential station, one who was an advocate for evangelical truth, rather than thrust him out to make way for an errorist in doctrine as well as in church order?

A further testimony to which he appeals is, that Calvin, in writing to *Ithavius*, a Polish Bishop, styles him " illustrious and Reverend Lord Bishop." He addresses him, "illustris et reverende Domine." The last word, which is equivalent to *sir*, Calvin addresses to the humblest curate to whom he writes. Of course no stress can be laid on that title. But what does the venerable Reformer say to this Polish dignitary? Urging him to give his influence decisively in favour of the Reformation, he writes to him in the following faithful language—a *part* of which only Bishop Ives quotes—" It is base and wicked for *you* to remain neutral, when God as with outstretched hand, calls you to defend his cause. Consider what place you occupy, and what burden has been laid upon you." This is proof enough that Calvin thought that *Ithavius* had been placed in his station by the providence of God, and that he was bound to employ all the influence and authority connected with that station for promoting the cause of truth; and certainly nothing more. I take for granted that Bishop Ives believes that the tyrant Nero was raised to the imperial throne by the providence of God; that, in that station, he had a great opportunity for doing good, if he had been inclined to improve it; and that any benevolent inhabitant of his dominions might have addressed his emperor in the very language addressed to *Ithavius*, without believing in the divine right of monarchy.

An extract of a letter from Calvin to the King of Poland, is also brought forward to show that he was an advocate for Prelacy. Let the passage which Bishop Ives refers to be seen in its connexion, and its worthlessness for his purpose, will be manifest to the most cursory reader. It is as follows:— " Finally, it is ambition and arrogance alone that have invented this Primacy which the Romanists hold up to us. The ancient Church did indeed institute **Patriarchates,** and also appointed certain primacies to each province, in order that, by this bond of concord, the Bishops might continue more united among themselves; just as if at the present day, one Archbishop were set over the kingdom of Poland; not to bear rule over the others, or to arrogate to himself authority of which the others are robbed; but for the sake of order, to hold the first place in Synods, and to cherish a holy union among his colleagues and brethren. Then there might be either provincial or city Bishops, to attend particularly to the preservation of order: inasmuch as nature dictates that, out of each college one should be chosen on whom the chief care should devolve. But possessing an office of moderate dignity, that is to the extent of a man's ability, is a different thing from embracing the whole world in unlimited jurisdiction."

Here it is evident that, by the "Ancient Church," Calvin meant, not the apostolic church; for *then* there were no *patriarchates*, as all agree; but the church as it stood in the fourth and fifth centuries. He thus fully explains this phrase in his letter to *Sadolet*, as well as in his *Institutes*. And it is no less evident that by the man in each college of ecclesiastics on whom the "chief care was to be devolved," he meant only a *standing moderator*, such as he describes in those extracts from his commentary, which I detailed in my last letter. And besides, as Calvin knew that prelacy was universally and firmly established in Poland, he was much more anxious to plead for the promotion of the doctrines and spirit of true religion in that country, than for pulling down its hierarchy. Hence he was disposed to treat the latter with indulgence, if the former might have free course.

But Bishop Ives seems to lay the greatest stress for proof of his assertion, on a statement found in *Strype's* "Memorials of Cranmer," p. 207; and in his "Life of Bishop *Parker*," pp. 69, 70. The story, as related by Strype, is, that *Bullinger and Calvin* and others, wrote a joint letter to king Edward, offering to make him their defender, and to have such bishops in their churches as there were in England. The story is a blind and incredible one. Let us see the letter, and we will then believe that such a communication was sent, and not till then. The truth is, Bonner and Gardiner were popish bishops, entirely out of favour during the reign of king Edward, and a letter directed to the king would be by no means likely to fall into their hands. Calvin is known to have kept up a constant correspondence with Archbishop Cranmer, as long as the latter lived. Cranmer consulted him frequently, sought his counsel on a variety of occasions, and requested his aid in conducting the affairs of the English Reformation. The Archbishop sent to Calvin the first draught of the English Liturgy, early in the reign of Edward, requesting his advice and criticism respecting it. Calvin returned it, saying that he found in it some *tolerabiles ineptias* (some tolerable fooleries) which he could wish might be corrected. This criticism was well received, and the Liturgy was corrected agreeably to his wishes. This fact is attested by Dr. *Heylin*, one of the bitterest opponents of Calvin, and of Presbyterianism, that ever lived. "The first Liturgy," says he, "was discontinued, and the second superinduced upon it, to give satisfaction unto Calvin's cavils, the curiosities of some, and the mistakes of others, his friends and followers." *History of the Presbyterians*, p. 12. 207. Dr. *Nichols*, also, the author of a Commentary on the Common Prayer, bears testimony to the same fact, in the following statement. "Four years afterwards the Book of Common Prayer underwent another review, wherein some ceremonies and usages were laid aside, and some new prayers added, at the instance of Mr. Calvin of Geneva, and Bucer, a foreign divine, who was invited to be a Professor at Cambridge." *Preface to his Comment*, p. 5.

The fact is, Cranmer and his coadjutors in the English Reformation, had to struggle with great difficulties. The Papists, on the one hand, assailed and reproached them for carrying the Reformation too far; while some of the most pious dignitaries, and others in the Church, thought it was not carried far enough. In these circumstances, Cranmer wrote often to the Reformers on the Continent, and sought advice and countenance from them, and to none more frequently than to Calvin who wrote, we are told, in return, much to encourage and animate Cranmer. Among other expressions of opinion, we are informed that Calvin blamed Bishops *Hooper* and *Latimer,* those decided friends of evangelical truth, for their persevering scruples respecting the *habits* or ecclesiastical *vestments,* which were then the subject of so much controversy. He gave it as his opinion that where the great and vital principles of the Gospel were at stake, it was bad policy for the friends of true religion to allow themselves to be alienated and divided by questions concerning clerical *dress,* or even the *external order* of the Church. The kind and friendly things of this nature which he so frequently uttered, were no doubt, misinterpreted, as indicating a more favourable opinion of the Prelacy of England, than he really entertained, or ever meant to express.

I shall trespass on your patience, Mr. Editor, only by making one statement more. Calvin was so far from ever alleging that the *Genevan* form of church government was adopted by him from *necessity* and not from *choice,* that he, on the contrary, steadfastly maintained that it was strictly agreeable to the word of God, and that which he felt himself bound, by obedience to Christ, to establish and defend. " Besides," says he, " that our conscience acquits us in the sight of God, the thing itself will answer for us in the sight of men. Nobody has yet appeared that could prove that we had *altered any one thing* which God has commanded, or that we have appointed *any new thing*, contrary to his word, or that we have *turned aside from the truth* to follow any evil opinion. On the contrary it is manifest that we have reformed our church MERELY BY GOD'S WORD, which is the *only rule* by which it is to be ordered, and lawfully defended. It is, indeed, an unpleasant work to alter what has been formerly in use, were it not that the order which God has once fixed must be esteemed by us as sacred and inviolable; insomuch, that if it has, for a time, been laid aside, it must of necessity, (and whatever the consequences should prove,) be restored again. No antiquity, no prescription of custom, may be allowed to be an obstacle in this case, that *the government of the church which God has appointed,* should not be perpetual, *since the Lord himself has once fixed it.*" *Epis. ad quendam Curatum—In Calvin. Epist. p.* 386.

Such are the testimonies which satisfy me that Calvin was a sincere and uniform advocate of Presbyterian church government, and that if he ever wished to introduce Prelacy into his church at Geneva, we must despair of establishing any fact by historical records. That Bishop Ives was a real believer in the truth of all that he asserted, I never entertained the least doubt. But I have as little doubt, that it is totally destitute of any solid foundation. Either Calvin had no such desire as the bishop ascribes to him, or he was one of the most weak and inconsistent men that ever breathed. *That* nobody ever thought him.

I am, Mr. Editor, yours respectfully,

SAMUEL MILLER.

PRINCETON, *Dec.* 6, 1841.

# ADDENDA.

The estimation in which the character and learning of Calvin have been held, may be seen from the following testimonies.

"He lived fifty four years, ten months, and seventeen days; half of which time he passed in the sacred ministry. His stature was of a middle size, his complexion dark and pallid, his eyes brilliant even till death, expressing the acuteness of his understanding. He lived nearly without sleep. His power of memory was almost incredible; and his judgment so sound, that his decisions often seemed almost oracular. In his words he was sparing; and he despised an artificial eloquence: yet was he an accomplished writer: and, by the accuracy of his mind, and his practice of dictating to an amanuensis, he attained to speak little differently from what he would have written. The consistency and uniformity of his doctrine, from first to last, are scarcely to be paralleled. Nature had formed him grave; yet in the intercourse of social life no one showed more suavity. He exercised great forbearance towards all such infirmities in others as are consistent with integrity—not overawing his weaker brethren: but towards flattery, and every species of insincerity, especially where religion was concerned, he was severe and indignant. He was naturally irritable: and this fault was increased by the excessive laboriousness of his life: yet the Spirit of God had taught him to govern both his temper and his tongue.—That so many and so great virtues both in public and in private life should have called forth against him many enemies, no one will wonder who duly considers what has ever befallen eminent men, both in sacred and profane history. Those enemies brand him as *a heretic:* but Christ suffered under the same reproach. He was *expelled*, say they from Geneva. True, he was, but he was solicited to return. He is charged with *ambition*, yea with aspiring at a new popedom. An extraordinary charge to be brought against a man who chose *his* kind of life, and in this state, in this church, which I might truly call the very seat of poverty. They say again that he *coveted wealth*. Yet all his worldly goods, including his library, which brought a high price, scarcely amounted to three hundred crowns. Well might he say in his preface to the book of Psalms, 'That I am not a lover of money, if I fail of persuading men while I live, my death will demonstrate.' How small his stipend was the senate knows: yet they can bear witness that, so far from being dissatisfied with it, he pertinaciously refused an increase when it was offered him. He delighted, forsooth, in *luxury* and indulgence! Let his labours answer the charge. What accusations will not some men bring against him? But no refutation of them is wanting to those persons who knew him while he lived; and they will want none, among posterity, with men of judgment who shall collect his character from his writings. Having given with good faith the history of his life and of his death, after sixteen years' observation of him, I feel myself warranted to declare, that in him was proposed to all men an illustrious example of the life and death of a Christian: so that it will be found as difficult to emulate, as it is easy to calumniate him."— *Beza.*

"It is impossible to refuse him the praise of vast knowledge, exquisite judgment, a penetration which is uncommon, a prodigious memory, and admirable temperance and sobriety ... Affairs public and private, ecclesiastical and civil, occupied him in succession, and often all together. Consulted from all quarters both at home and abroad; carrying on a correspondence with all the churches and all the learned men of Europe, with the princes and other persons of high distinction, who had embraced the reformed religion; it seems almost inconceivable how one man could be capable of so many things, and how he should not sink under the weight of the business which pressed upon him. The enemy of all pomp; modest in his whole deportment; perfectly disinterested and generous, and even entertaining a contempt for riches;

he made himself not less respected for the qualities of his heart, than admired for the powers of his understanding. When the council wished to make him a present of five and twenty crowns on occasion of his continued illness, he refused to accept it; because, he said, since he then rendered no service to the church, so far from meriting any extraordinary recompense he felt scruples about receiving his ordinary stipend: and a few days before his death he absolutely refused a part of his appointments which had become due . . . He always presided in the company of pastors. Without envy they saw him, by reason of his rare merit, which raised him far above all his colleagues, occupy the first place . . . . When his frequent illnesses prevented his being regularly present among them, they had requested Beza to supply his place. A few days after Calvin's death, Beza declined this service, and at the same time recommended to them not in future to entrust an office of such importance permanently to any individual—safely as it might have been committed to Calvin, and due as it justly was to his services—. . . but rather to choose a fresh moderator every year, who should simply be considered as *primus inter pares*—presiding among his equals. This proposition was unanimously approved, and Beza himself notwithstanding the pleas on which he would have been excused, was immediately chosen the first moderator, as possessing all the requisite qualifications: and the choice was sanctioned by the council."—*Spon's History of Geneva.*

"This (his superiority to the love of money) is one of the most extraordinary victories virtue and magnanimity can obtain over nature, even in those who are ministers of the gospel. Calvin has left behind him many who imitated him in his active life, his zeal and affection for the cause; they employ their voices, their pens, their steps and solicitations, for the advancement of the kingdom of God, but then they take care not to forget themselves, and are, generally speaking, a demonstration that the church is a bountiful mother, and that nothing is lost in her service.... Such a will as this of Calvin, and such a disinterestedness, is a thing so very extraordinary, as might make even those who cast their eyes on the philosophers of Greece say of him, 'I have not found so great faith, no not in Israel.' When Calvin was taking his leave of those of Strasburg, in order to return to Geneva, they offered to continue his freedom, and the revenue of a prebend they had assigned him: he accepted the first, but rejected the latter.... He carried one of his brothers with him to Geneva, without ever thinking of advancing him to any honours, as others would have done with his great credit... Even his enemies say he had him taught the trade of a book-binder, which he exercised all his life."—*Bayle.*

"We should be injurious unto virtue itself,

if we did derogate from them whom their industry hath made great. Two things of principal moment there are, which have deservedly procured him honour throughout the world: the one his exceeding pains in composing the Institutions of Christian Religion, the other his no less industrious travails for exposition of holy scripture, according unto the same institutions. In which two things whosoever they were that after him bestowed their labour, he gained the advantage of prejudice against them if they gainsayed, and of glory above them if they consented."—*Hooker.*

"After the holy scriptures, I exhort the students to read the Commentaries of Calvin: ... for I tell them that he is incomparable in the interpretation of scripture; and that his Commentaries ought to be held in greater estimation than all that is delivered to us in the writings of the ancient Christian fathers: so that, in a certain eminent spirit of prophecy, I give the preeminence to him beyond most others, indeed beyond them all. I add, that, with regard to what belongs to common places, his Institutes must be read after the Catechism, as a more ample interpretation. But to all this I subjoin the remark, that they must be perused with cautious choice, like all other human compositions."—*Arminius.*

**THE END.**

www.ingramcontent.com/pod-product-compliance
Lightning Source LLC
Chambersburg PA
CBHW070927160426
43193CB00011B/1599